Let's Talk About Aging Parents

———

"Being thrust into the role of caregiver for an aging parent (or two) can be challenging, overwhelming even. There are so many questions and so much fear. Thankfully, Laura Tamblyn Watts provides many of the answers—guiding us from 'The Talk' about moving from the family home to a care home, to the sensitive discussion about whether it's time to stop driving, to the joys of toileting. This is a book whose practical tips will save you many a sleepless night."
—ANDRÉ PICARD, **health columnist for** *The Globe and Mail* **and author of** *Neglected No More: The Urgent Need To Improve The Lives of Canada's Elders in the Wake of a Pandemic*

"As an international leader in aging, Laura Tamblyn Watts invites us to join her on a journey supporting the older adults in our lives. Her vital questions and practical tips help us navigate caregiving with grace, humor, dignity, love, and joy. As I discuss what's next with my own aging mother, this book is a lifeline filled with sample scripts and pragmatic charts. I wholeheartedly recommend this guide to the current and next generations of care providers and family members."
—BONNIE BRANDL, **founder and former director of the National Clearinghouse on Abuse in Later Life (NCALL)**

"With her characteristic wit and panache, Laura Tamblyn Watts had me laughing, shouting, weeping, and reading with my jaw dropped. She tells real, relatable stories and offers concrete actions that all of us can take. I can't wait to share this book with my friends and family."
—GREGOR SNEDDON, **executive director of HelpAge Canada**

"This is a profound, astute book that resonates with readers from all walks of life. It provides unique insights on our aging population and brings the realities so many families are facing to the surface, offering a strong foundation for engaging in a conversation that we all need to have. It's real, it hits home, and it's on point."
—KAHIR LALJI, certified professional gerontologist, vice chair of HelpAge Canada, and provincial director of government relations and programs at United Way British Columbia

"This book comes at a significant time as we work toward providing better support for our aging population, and as a new caregiver myself, I relate very strongly to the subjects it covers. Tamblyn Watts includes all the topics that are vitally important to anyone who is caring for an aging parent. She navigates challenging issues with eloquence, demonstrating profound empathy and understanding on each page."
—ALEX MIHAILIDIS, scientific director of AGE-WELL and professor at the University of Toronto

Let's Talk About Aging Parents

A Real-Life Guide to Solving Problems with 27 Essential Conversations

LAURA TAMBLYN WATTS

Foreword by DEBRA WHITMAN,
Chief Public Policy Officer, AARP

THE EXPERIMENT

NEW YORK

The Experiment, LLC
220 East 23rd Street, Suite 600
New York, NY 10010-4658
theexperimentpublishing.com

This book contains the opinions and ideas of its author. It is intended to provide helpful and informative material on the subjects addressed in the book. It is sold with the understanding that the author and publisher are not engaged in rendering medical, health, or any other kind of personal professional services in the book. The author and publisher specifically disclaim all responsibility for any liability, loss, or risk—personal or otherwise—that is incurred as a consequence, directly or indirectly, of the use and application of any of the contents of this book.

THE EXPERIMENT and its colophon are registered trademarks of The Experiment, LLC. Many of the designations used by manufacturers and sellers to distinguish their products are claimed as trademarks. Where those designations appear in this book and The Experiment was aware of a trademark claim, the designations have been capitalized.

The Experiment's books are available at special discounts when purchased in bulk for premiums and sales promotions as well as for fundraising or educational use. For details, contact us at info@theexperimentpublishing.com.

Library of Congress Cataloging-in-Publication Data

Names: Tamblyn Watts, Laura, author. | Whitman, Debra B., writer of
    foreword.
Title: Let's talk about aging parents : a real-life guide to solving
    problems with 27 essential conversations / Laura Tamblyn Watts ;
    foreword by Debra Whitman, Chief Public Policy Officer, AARP
Description: New York : The Experiment, [2024] | Includes bibliographical
    references and index.
Identifiers: LCCN 2023058429 (print) | LCCN 2023058430 (ebook) | ISBN
    9781615198023 (paperback) | ISBN 9781615198030 (ebook)
Subjects: LCSH: Aging parents--Care. | Adult children of aging parents.
Classification: LCC HQ1063.6 .T36 2024 (print) | LCC HQ1063.6 (ebook) |
    DDC 306.874084/6--dc23/eng/20240201
LC record available at https://lccn.loc.gov/2023058429
LC ebook record available at https://lccn.loc.gov/2023058430

ISBN 978-1-61519-802-3
Ebook ISBN 978-1-61519-803-0

Cover and text design by Jack Dunnington
Author photo by Andrea Stenson

Manufactured in the United States of America

First printing April 2024
10 9 8 7 6 5 4 3 2 1

To my beloved husband, Michael Tamblyn. You are my everything. I adore you. Thank you for your late-night edits, your constant encouragement, and your mantra, "Writers write. Authors finish." It's finished.

And to my parents, Tanya and Sandy McKay, who had absolutely no idea I was writing this book until just now. Thanks for everything. You are the best parents ever, with a generous sense of humor and forgiveness. This book is not *about you. I swear.*

Contents

PART 1
The house, home care, and moving out

PART 2
Mental capacity, power of attorney, and safety

PART 3
Love, loss, and hopefully some laughs

PART 4
Health, hearing issues, and horrible driving

Foreword

by Debra Whitman, Chief Public Policy Officer, AARP

A few months ago, a good friend from high school called me. Kim told me that her mom, Jill, had been out walking the dog when a squirrel crossed their path and the dog tried to chase it. Jill was thrown off-balance and fell hard on the ground, fracturing her pelvis in four places and breaking her shoulder. She went to the emergency room, then spent several days in the ICU before transferring to a rehabilitation facility. By the time Kim called me, Jill was stable. But a lot had changed. Jill, who just a week earlier had been a fit and independent woman in her seventies, could now do very little on her own.

Kim and I talked through where she could find help and resources for Jill and how important it was to make Jill's house safe and accessible so she could eventually come home. Kim moved to Idaho from Washington state to help, and she lived with Jill for the next two months, calling her own kids nightly to check in. She made sure Jill visited a rehabilitation specialist twice a week and did her exercises every day. After a couple months, Jill regained nearly all her mobility. By the time Kim left, she told me that Jill was following three key rules they developed together: Keep moving but never rush, ask for help if needed, and stay hydrated and fed.

I was happy to be on Kim's call list for moral and practical support, but I wish Kim and her family would have had a book like *Let's Talk About Aging Parents*—not just for after Jill's accident, but in the months and years before—to help them have the conversations we all need to start having with our aging relatives.

In Laura's wonderful and wise book, she has pulled off the impossible: making some very tough issues more manageable while allowing us to laugh along the way.

I love a checklist, and this book has many. It will guide you through everything from helping your parent downsize to finding long-term care that they are happy with to creating activities that keep them connected with grandkids. Laura doesn't shy away from the most awkward issues: divorce and new relationships, financial scams, incontinence. For some people, even discussing the possibility of declining capacity is taboo, and Laura suggests different approaches to these conversations. She helps us prioritize listening so that no matter how we frame a discussion, we always offer our parents the sensitivity and understanding they need and deserve.

She also shows us how to be gentle with ourselves and realistic about what is possible. It's complicated to work with other family members when everyone wants to do something different (and some opt for not helping at all), and it's easy to feel guilty about never doing enough or never doing it right. Laura speaks to these challenges in ways I found very reassuring.

I've known Laura for many years and admire her commitment to making the world a better place for older people. She started CanAge from scratch in 2019 and quickly turned it into one of the most innovative and influential advocacy organizations in the world. That same compassion and pragmatism comes through in her book, but so does her sense of fun. I can think of no better companion for difficult conversations than Laura.

Now, when a friend calls me to say their mom has fallen and broken a hip or their dad is starting to seem confused, I can tell them to turn to *Let's Talk About Aging Parents*. And of course, I'll refer to it myself. Although I have spent most of my career thinking about what happens to our bodies, minds, and money as we age, I can still feel unprepared to discuss these things with those closest to me. My parents are now in their eighties and (mostly) healthy and mobile. Recently, I began asking them questions about their own lives and what they wanted for their future: How long will they feel they can continue to drive safely? What will we do if they need care? What are their funeral wishes? At times, our discussions have been nearly as uncomfortable for us as "the talk" they had with me when I was a teenager. It would have been nice to have a script to help ease into these issues. Now, thanks to Laura, I do!

One of the messages that Laura's book really brings home is the importance of asking the older people in our lives what they want and truly listening to their answers. We can learn a lot. When I talked to my mother about her funeral preferences, she initially said she would be fine with anything my brother and I wanted. But after I prodded her, assuring her that I really did want to know, she gave me a rich description of her wishes. My mother has lived for the last fifty years in a small town in eastern Washington but plans to be buried in my father's family plot on the other side of the state. She told me how important it is to her that there be memorials both in her home church and at the grave site, so that her friends and family will all be able to attend, no matter where they live. Assuring her that we will honor these wishes seemed to give her some comfort.

I appreciated the clarity I came away with after that conversation, which brought my mother and me even closer. But as many of us know, things don't always go so smoothly. Understanding what our parents want may mean supporting decisions that we don't fully agree with. Physical and mental capacity changes as a person ages, but older people still have the right to determine where and with whom they live, their social life and physical activities, and what kind of care they do or do not wish to receive. We don't stop wanting to make decisions for ourselves just because we've reached a certain birthday. Those of us aiming to support older relatives need to remember this. We may not agree that a peanut butter sandwich is the best dinner for our parent, but if they want it and it doesn't put them in danger of choking, they should enjoy their peanut butter sandwich!

Finally, this book isn't just about getting better at talking with our older family members. All of us are getting older. As I move into my second fifty, *Let's Talk About Aging Parents* will help me plan for my own future—and I hope, when the time comes, I'll be more open to my children having some tough conversations with me. I want those talks to be good for us all. I want us to be honest but loving, to be as gentle or firm as we need to be, and to be able to laugh whenever we can. This book is all about making that possible.

DEBRA WHITMAN is AARP's chief public policy officer. An economist, expert on aging issues, and author of the forthcoming book *The Second Fifty: Answers to the 7 Big Questions of Midlife and Beyond*, she leads her team in all aspects of policy development, analysis, research, and global thought leadership to help communities, lawmakers, and the private sector improve our lives as we age.

Introduction

If you have an aging adult in your life, you might be familiar with this scenario: It's 3:00 AM. You're lying in bed, worrying, a million thoughts going through your mind. Your dad's memory isn't as good as it used to be. Your mom isn't getting around so well anymore. How do you tell them it might be time to make some changes? How do you make sure they're safe and secure?

And how do you do that without getting your head chewed off for stepping into their life when your advice isn't welcome? When your parent has always been a proud, independent person, and you're worried that pushing too hard might just make things worse? Or, less commonly, when your parent just says, "I'll do whatever you want," but you frankly have no clue what the best solution is, and you're worried whatever you decide may also mean really messing up your own life?

It gets even more chaotic when you sprinkle in some extra relatives and top the whole thing off with your other life responsibilities. How do you deal with the bossy older sibling who swoops in once a year, orders everyone around, then zips away on a flight forty-eight hours later? Or the younger failure-to-launch sibling who's sponging off your great aunt who probably can't afford it? How do you keep your head on straight when your spouse hates your parents, your sister keeps texting you about what she thinks *you* should do about Mom, and you still have that presentation for work to get done? Add the yard work you've been putting off, kids or dogs or (laughably) that yoga class you swear you're going to get to this week, and you've got the situation that so many of us are experiencing.

Instead of tying yourself into emotional knots about all this, let's get started with some solutions, laughs, and practical advice on how to get through life with an aging parent, without losing your cool (or your mind).

We're going to learn about the practical stuff: How to talk to your parent about whether they should be moving out of that three-story townhouse with the narrow, slippery stairs. About whether your dad should really be driving when he's essentially blind. About the fact that no, you're not mumbling . . . but maybe your mom needs hearing aids. We're going to figure out the best ways to get everyone to sit down and have a talk about who's going to make decisions if your parent gets sick and can't make their own choices—and whether it's really a good idea to give all eight kids equal powers of attorney (pro tip: no!). Here are the ins and outs of dealing with your dad's "new best friend" who's moved into his house and convinced your dad not to talk to you or handling those half-step-twice-removed family members who have suddenly developed a new affection for your ailing cousin and her fully paid off house in the city. And the big one: dementia. (Except when it isn't dementia and is actually something else, which is often.)

This book is for you whether you live across the country from your parent or right next door. Whether you're involved in their life every day or haven't been in contact for years. Whether you're an only child or one of twelve kids. It's also for you even if the older adult in your life isn't actually your mom or dad—I use "parent" to keep things simple, but you can also work with this advice if you're caring for a grandparent, another extended relative, or an elderly neighbor who's become your best friend. If your family has issues related to mental health, addiction, abuse or neglect, estrangement, an "unsuccessful son in the basement," second or third marriages, divorces, financial strains, or squabbling siblings . . . welcome to the club! That just makes you normal.

As we try to support aging parents, it's really easy to fall into one of two approaches: "Do what I say" or the always-popular "I wash my hands of this." I'd humbly suggest that neither approach works well for *anyone*, but especially for our parents. We get tangled up in coils of outgrown kid-love, echoes of teenage defensiveness, and "I'm a grown-up now" adulthood, and it doesn't matter how old we are—these relationships are tricky, layered, and fraught with emotion. Throughout this book, I'm going to encourage you to look beyond those two black-and-white options and just do the best you can as one imperfect human looking after another.

So, grab your beverage of choice. Be prepared to laugh. And maybe to take notes (scribble on these pages if you like). I'll warn you—caring for an aging parent is an art, not a science. (Except when it is actually medical science, which we'll get into.) Sometimes there won't be any good answers, but I'll at least help you learn to ask the right questions.

Let's get into it. After all, we aren't getting any younger.

LTW

PART 1

The house, home care, and moving out

1

Is my parent's home ready for them to age in place?

Your parent probably wants to stay in their home as they age—depending on the study you look at, between 75 and 90 percent[1] of older adults feel this way. And you likely agree with them, unless for some reason you love the idea of living with your mom again in your forties, only this time you're the one nagging her to do the dishes. But unfortunately, those desires don't always line up with reality. Only 10 percent of North American homes meet the very basic "aging-ready" standards of a step-free entryway, a first-floor bedroom and bathroom, and at least one bathroom-accessibility feature (like a grab bar or shower seat).[2]

This means if your parent doesn't want to move, and *you* don't want them to move either, you're probably going to need to work together on getting their living space prepared for them to stay. Age-proofing is similar to child-proofing: You'll be looking at each room of your parent's home from a new perspective to identify concerns like trip hazards or burn risks.

Some homes have structural issues that make them especially difficult to live in. Stairs are an obvious issue, but even single-level apartments can have uneven walkways and long hikes to reach elevators, garages, and laundry facilities. If that's your parent's situation, you'll need to be realistic about what can and can't be fixed, and you may need to reconsider a move to a more aging-friendly home.

There is such a thing as a professional aging-in-place safety assessment—one of these services looks at two hundred and forty markers around the home's full interior and exterior, and it comes with a complete summary of recommendations, plus referrals to pre-vetted contractors.[3] I've never used one of these, but it doesn't sound like a bad idea if you can afford it. For the DIY version, read on!

All around the house

GRAB BARS AND BANISTERS

Falling is one of the worst things that can happen to an older adult. If your parent falls and breaks their hip, their chance of dying within the next year is about 20 percent, increasing to around 40 percent in the next year and a half to two years.[4] Many people who survive still don't recover their baseline independence and function.[5] So, avoiding falls is key, and here's how to help with that.

Good: Install grab bars in all bathrooms, with a vertical bar outside each shower and at least one angled bar inside. Get banisters on both sides of all stairs so your parent can hold on with two hands.

Better: Install grab bars by all toilets, your parent's favorite chairs, and their bed. Put horizontal banisters along hallways.

Best: Fill your parent's house with grab bars and banisters! I'm only sort of kidding, but it's worthwhile having them next to front and back doors, both inside and outside. This is helpful to avoid slipping when it's wet outside, while wrestling with groceries, or when bracing against incoming puppies and grandchildren. (While you're thinking about the entryways, consider a seat to make putting on and taking off outdoor gear easier.) Also add banisters on the porch or back deck.

Cost: $
Grab bars themselves aren't particularly expensive, but depending on how handy you and your family are, they may require professional installation.

HANDLES

Approximately 50 percent of people aged sixty-five and older deal with arthritis.[6] Add on age-related issues with grip strength and hand steadiness, and opening and closing doors and cabinets becomes a real challenge. Round or oval-shaped door knobs can be especially painful and hard to use for many seniors. The easy solution: Replace door knobs with lever handles throughout your parent's home. Replace sink handles, too, since dripping taps lead to floods.

Good: Lever handles are cheap! End of story—no "better" or "best" here.

Cost: $

These handles can be inexpensive, but you can splurge on a wide variety of finishes and designs. You don't need a professional for this one—knowing what a screwdriver is should be adequate.

FLOORS, CARPETS, AND RUGS

There are different schools of thought about how to age-proof your parent's floors. Floor surfaces can be slippery compared to carpet, but they can also be too "grabby." ("Friction-y"? There has to be a better word.) This one really depends on individual needs, but I can tell you that throw rugs, polished concrete floors, and uneven rock surfaces (including those pebbly things you can install in the shower) are bad.

Good: Get rid of floor rugs in the areas your parent uses the most. If they're gorgeous rugs with sentimental value, you can display them hanging on the wall instead! And if your parent simply must have a throw rug, make sure it has a non-slip backing, preferably attached rather than with a separate liner.

Better: If falling is a concern, replace polished concrete floors, slippery tile, or wood with low-pile carpeting. Make sure the carpet's underlay is firm, not squishy and soft. Of course, if your parent uses an assistive device like a wheelchair or walker, carpeting may not be an option. Also, install high-friction or grip tiling in bathrooms, kitchens, and laundry rooms.

Best: Let your parent's interior design desires run wild—if shag carpeting makes their life worth living, then work around it however you can, possibly by installing a hard plastic mat in particular areas where your parent walks or rolls around the most. Consider changing the tires on walkers or rollators to make travel on low-pile carpeting easier. You can look for new types of engineered hardwood, tile, and other flooring that sometimes come in non-slip varieties.

Cost: $$

Room size and shape, carpet material, furniture removal, and installation will all be factors in flooring costs. You'll almost certainly need a professional here, and you should get at least three bids as prices can vary. Sometimes stores have "remnant" sales where you can buy pre-cut portions of carpeting for less, which can be useful for smaller spaces.

STORAGE

In bathrooms, kitchens, closets, and entryways, pull-out drawers on easy slides can make a big difference. Hard-to-open drawers create clutter if your parent leaves things lying around to avoid fighting with the sticky antique dresser drawer, and that mess can then turn into tripping hazards—plus, it can be dangerous if the impossible drawer finally flies out and drops onto their feet. For best results, your parent shouldn't need to reach up to access storage, since that can lead to falls or bonks on the head.

Good: Go to a DIY home renovation store like IKEA (hot tip: check the children's section) and find a bedroom wardrobe with easy-to-open drawers and new drawers for the kitchen. While you're working on the kitchen, move any hanging storage (like racks of pots and pans) to eye level or lower.

Better: Add pull-out inserts to kitchen and bathroom cabinets. If applicable, redo the drawers in the front and back entryways as well.

Best: Have someone who specializes in age-friendly designs help you reorganize your parent's storage.

Cost: $–$$

This varies depending on cabinet size. Even if you can update only some of the storage in your parent's house, every little bit helps!

The bedroom

By now, we know that stairs are the enemy, so ideally everything your parent needs would be on one floor (with the basement and upstairs used for guests and storage). But if you can't make that happen, it's most important for your parent's bedroom to be on the main floor.

Ideally, this would be a spacious master bedroom with a connecting en suite bathroom. Not an option? Think about any rooms in your parent's house that aren't currently being used much, paying attention to the ones closest to a bathroom. Do they really need that formal dining room anymore? Could the den be converted? It won't be perfect, but if you can put in a twin bed (or, even better, a folding Murphy bed), that'll do. You could even install a folding door or room divider for privacy.

Whatever the bedroom ends up looking like, here are a few other tips.

- Reduce the amount of furniture so it's easier for your parent to move around.
- If they're sharing a bed, consider getting two sets of covers, European-style (for example, two twin sheets on a king-size bed). This prevents getting twisted and trapped in bed (or, if you're my husband, getting your covers stolen by your wife!).
- Update bedside lighting by reducing the number of large or wobbly lamps. Instead, install adjustable lights that are fixed to the wall and easy to turn on and off. You could even set up an "everything on/off" switch by the bed to prevent scrambling around in the dark.

The bathroom

THE SHOWER

Just like the bedroom, having a bathroom on the main floor is key. Ideally, this should include a walk-in (or roll-in in case your parent needs assistive devices) shower. Climbing over a tub lip is a sure way to fall, and even showers that you have to step up and into aren't ideal. Make sure the shower door is easy to open, too.

I'm a big fan of showers that have a good, solid seat (not one of those teeny corner things). I also like a place to lift your leg while seated—this can be achieved with a small stool that has suction cups on the legs. A handheld showerhead is always great, too.

Get non-slip flooring or make sure any bath mat is rubber-backed and non-slip. On the outside of the shower, put towel racks close at hand and don't forget about the grab bars I suggested earlier.

THE TOILET

You'll want a high toilet if possible—the old low ones are terrible! If you can't buy a new one, add a "lift" (with hired help, unless you're particularly handy) to raise an existing toilet up from the bottom.

You can also explore raised toilet seats and frames. When it comes to the seat, make sure that it can fit securely on top of the existing toilet seat without sliding around. Some versions have "arms" for added support while getting on or off the toilet, and some of those arms can be adjusted based on bum size.

Make sure the toilet paper roll is easy to reach—when the roll is installed on the side of the toilet, it can be awkward to grasp, so in front is best. You can leave the built-in roll where it is and buy a portable toilet paper holder that can be moved around as needed. You might also want to find an accessible place for adult-size flushable wet wipes.

If you want to be really fancy, you can buy all kinds of bidets that attach to an existing toilet. Some have functions that can wash, dry, and even heat the seat!

The kitchen

THE COUNTERS

Countertops should be easy to see, so if you're installing new ones, pick a material that's a different color than cabinets and flooring—or put a colored material like duct tape on the edges of existing counters. They also shouldn't have any sharp edges, so either get them rounded off by a craftsperson or add detachable "edge bumpers" (sometimes these are sold for toddlers).

If your parent uses a wheelchair or sits to do many tasks, they could benefit from some lower counter areas—thirty inches high rather than the standard thirty-six. You could include gaps to pull in a chair or assistive device, too.

THE OVEN AND STOVETOP

If at all possible, get rid of the gas stove. If your parent becomes more forgetful as they age, significant hazards can occur if the stove gets left on. Automatic shut-off ovens and stovetops are great—these can come built in or be added to an existing appliance. (For bonus points, get an electric grill for the backyard, too.) Stick to good old knobs instead of induction countertops, since many seniors can find induction interfaces hard to manipulate.

THE REFRIGERATOR

It may be helpful to get a fridge and freezer that's split down the middle (rather than a top and bottom drawer) or separate units to cut down on bending over. In the latter case, I recommend getting different-colored appliances or putting different things on them (like magnets or grandkids' art) so they're easy to tell apart.

I also appreciate that some newer fridges have clear glass fronts, which can visually remind your parent to eat or purchase more food. Even a glass-fronted bar fridge can be helpful.

THE SINK

A sprayer-style faucet that's flexible and easy to maneuver makes washing up much more accessible, and it's often inexpensive. For safety, make sure the heat adjustment on the water is warm rather than scalding, particularly if your parent has hand strength issues or cognitive impairment. There are sinks with adjustable heights, or as with the countertops, you could consider leaving the area underneath open for seated dishwashing.

THE COOKING TOOLS

Depending on your parent's cognitive ability, consider getting shelves with open or glass fronts so they can immediately see the tools they need. Put dangerous or too-heavy objects like fondue pots and gas or cast-iron pans in storage, then figure out what your parent uses most and make those items easily accessible.

Purchase an easy-grip or automatic can opener and look for other easy-grip or simple-to-hold tools that have large wooden or silicone handles. You can also buy specific "elder-friendly" dishes and silverware.

The living room

Depending on your parent's needs, you can reorganize this space to make room for parking assistive devices like rollators, or you can add a hook to rest a cane. No matter what, get cords out of the way—ideally hidden behind furniture and up against the wall.

Hopefully your parent already has a favorite comfy chair, but if you're buying new furniture, consider a recliner with a pop-out footrest. This can act as double duty for a place to sleep if your parent needs to keep their head or feet elevated due to illness.

If your parent has hearing loss, consider buying Bluetooth headphones or hearing aids that connect to the TV. (See chapter 22 for more on hearing issues.)

The laundry room

Again, this belongs on the main floor—no carrying heavy hampers of clothes up and down the stairs. If that's not possible, think about a laundry chute to remove one half of the trip.

High-profile washers and dryers that load from the front rather than the top are best. For people with hearing loss, you'll either want something with a loud "laundry's done" alarm or a machine that connects to a device like a phone that can flash a light.

The outside

Hearing can also be an issue for the front door, so there are doorbells that cause a phone to ring or flash. Consider putting in ramps or stone inclines (plus handrails!) leading into doorways. "Gap protectors" that turn a step into an incline are fairly inexpensive.

If there's a backyard, consider having it fenced in if you're worried about your parent wandering. Make sure any walkways are non-slip.

If your parent is a gardener, put in raised garden beds—you can buy them premade or get them custom-made, and they're about hip- to waist-high. Or put pots and containers on existing raised surfaces. Make sure that there is a lightweight garden hose close by, and perhaps even put in automatic sprinklers with shutoff valves. You can also buy long-handled tools for pet-poop disposal and weeding.

This chapter involves much more action than words (if only we could just talk the house into becoming an aging-in-place paradise!), but of course, it's important to take your parent's specific needs and tastes into account every step of the way. The next chapter includes scripts on getting your parent help at home, which can also be a useful starting point for convincing them that no, they shouldn't just keep everything as it is in their condo full of tripping hazards. Good luck and have fun—who knows, maybe you'll discover a passion for interior decorating along the way!

2

Does my parent need help around the house?

If you're reading this book, the answer is probably "yes," or perhaps "soon." It might not be a lot of help right now, but a bit of planning and budgeting can stop you from scrambling without a plan or resources when your parent needs more assistance later. When you go through this section, start using it as a tool to think about whether or not they can really manage around the house, or whether the answer is leaning more toward them moving into some type of independent or retirement living. But let's start with help at home first.

I'm giving you the heads-up—this can be a triggering conversation for some older parents. Whether you have a traditional "Dad takes care of the outside of the house and fixes things, while Mom takes care of the inside of the house and cooks" setup, or whether one parent handles construction *and* makes cakes while the other is a world-famous topiary artist, there is a lot of self-worth tied up in what someone does around the house.

Timing can be key to a successful discussion. Start the conversation ahead of time if there will be seasonal tasks that need doing, such as planting bulbs, putting up holiday lights, or spring cleaning. And don't bring it up when your parent is already dealing with a broken appliance and tensions are running high—find a time when everyone is calm and relaxed if possible.

Signs it's time to have the conversation

Your parent has new or worsening medical issues: Multiple sclerosis (MS), Parkinson's, and dementia are some big ones to watch out for—if you suspect any of these three conditions, even without a formal diagnosis, you should already be starting the conversation. Arthritis is also serious business that can lead to a downward spiral of pain and difficulty moving. Finally, once your parent has had a bad fall, particularly if they break something like a hip, they will need help, fast.

Your parent has issues getting around: They might be having trouble getting in and out of their bed or lounge chair. Picking something up off the floor could require a handle for support, a wobble when leaning down, and an "oof" when rising back up. Or they may need to hold on to a wall or chair and use countertops to keep themselves upright. Overall, falling is incredibly dangerous, and if your parent loses their balance just moving around at home, they need some assistance.

Things look wrong: If your parent has always shared my dislike of scrubbing, perhaps you won't notice changes as much. But if the garden looks untended when it's usually pristine or the bathrooms are gritty and it's a real shock, then it's time. Laundry is heavy and hard to manage, too, so if your parent looks like they've been sleeping in their clothes or their shirts are stained, that's a sign something isn't right.

Things smell wrong: When you open your parent's fridge, does it have expired food inside? (For those with vision or memory issues, it can be hard to read expiration dates or remember when things go "off.") Or does the bathroom, or your parent, smell funny? (Especially pay attention to urine scents.)

Stuff isn't working: As a procrastinator myself, I'm not talking about avoidant behavior, but rather key everyday things being out of order. Clocks not being set. The TV or internet is not working. The wacky avoidance techniques for jobs like a stuck door (just use the other one!) or a rotten step (just make sure you avoid it!). Also keep an eye out for crazy household fixes, like a tennis racket blocking squirrels from coming down the fireplace or a beaded necklace holding a window shut.

Preparing for the conversation

Here are some questions to probe with before you actually bring up the subject of help around the house.

WHAT JOBS DO THEY LOVE OR IDENTIFY WITH?

Make a list of the jobs your parent likes, the ones that are key to their dignity and lifestyle.

Are they a gardener? They may accept some help with the heavy lifting and mulch spreading so they can focus on the jobs they enjoy more. Are they a dog person whose daily long walks are a big part of staying healthy or connecting with their social group? If getting down the front steps becomes tougher, you could see about getting railings or a ramp installed.

Overall, try to preserve the important stuff by identifying the hard or dangerous parts of those activities, then working on ways they can maintain the roles they really like.

WHAT JOBS DO THEY COMPLAIN ABOUT OR DOWNRIGHT HATE?

Sometimes, the easiest way to get your parent to accept help is to get rid of something they dislike.

My mother hates grocery shopping—the minute I turned sixteen, she handed me the car keys and told me that groceries were now my job in exchange for borrowing her car. She also hates ironing so much that she'd hide the holiday shortbread in the ironing basket on the rationale that no one would ever look through it. (You were wrong about that, Mom—I'm fine with ironing and your shortbread is delicious. Sorry there wasn't any for the holiday guests . . .)

In the absence of obvious signs like these, start by casually asking what your parent doesn't like doing. Is it cleaning the bathrooms? Putting away the laundry? Bending over to do the lawn edging? Taking the car to the shop?

THE HOUSEHOLD TASKS CHECKLIST

Here's a list of tasks to make thinking through all the options easier. First, identify which ones you or your family and friends can take off their plate. Then, figure out those that likely require outside volunteers or paid help.

Task	Notes	Which family member or friend can help?	Should we find a volunteer or hire someone?
OUTDOOR			
Lawn care	Seasonal and ongoing		
Gardening	Seasonal and ongoing		
Seasonal HVAC help	Furnace, air conditioner, etc.		
Grocery purchasing and delivery			
Other errands			
INDOOR			
Odd jobs and fixes	Hanging up pictures, cleaning ceiling fans, etc.		
Cooking			
Washing and putting away dishes			
Putting away groceries			
Assembling purchased items	Like IKEA furniture		

Task	Notes	Which family member or friend can help?	Should we find a volunteer or hire someone?
Cleaning and tidying			
Decluttering			
Laundry and dry cleaning			
Errand list-making			
Electronics help			
Bed making and linen changing			

THEIR BODY

Task	Notes	Which family member or friend can help?	Should we find a volunteer or hire someone?
Personal grooming	Hair care, skin care, nails, spa stuff		
Health and dental appointments			
Buying clothing and footwear			
Exercise	Maybe a class or personal trainer?		
Massage, physio, or occupational therapy			

PET CARE

Task	Notes	Which family member or friend can help?	Should we find a volunteer or hire someone?
Dog walking			
Emptying litter boxes or backyard poop cleanup			

Task	Notes	Which family member or friend can help?	Should we find a volunteer or hire someone?
Grooming and bathing	Including tick checks—they're very hard to see!		
Vet trips			
Pet sitting			
SEASONAL OR OCCASIONAL			
Vacation home maintenance			
Pool or hot tub maintenance			
Holiday or party decorating			
Special occasion food preparation			
Pre-hosting help	Polishing the silver, getting any special dishware from wherever it's hidden, setting the table, serving food		
OTHER			
Driving and transportation (see chapter 27)			
Automotive maintenance			
Library book returns			

WHOM DO THEY TRUST AND WHAT CAN THEY AFFORD?

Now that you know what kind of tasks you're dealing with, do some research before jumping into the conversation. Depending on where you live and what you can afford, finding support can be difficult, so be prepared to spend some time digging.

If your parent is already connected to a faith group, a community center, or a club, that can be a good place to start. If they need help getting meals and their faith group has a dinner every Wednesday night, have those details handy—and maybe in the process, find out if this same group regularly offers takeaway dinners. Check out local resources that offer free services, too. If you're comfortable using credentialed apps or websites, you could make a list of people and volunteer to reach out to them.

As you search, find out prices. Some parents may have real cost constraints. Others may have the funds but haven't got their heads around starting to need help, and the hourly or contract costs may seem shocking—particularly if their last point of reference was finding a babysitter to take care of you for a buck an hour forty years ago.

Strategies for having the conversation

THE GENTLE "REFERRAL" APPROACH

One nonthreatening way to begin is by appealing to your parent's expertise. It might look like this:

> "Hey, Aunt Olga—I've been making a list of things I would like help with around the house, and I'm looking for referrals. Do you have a cleaning service you like? Or do you know someone who does good lawn and gardening care?"

Or like this:

> "Dad, I'm finding that I need help installing electronics whenever I buy a new TV or computer. I'd really love to have someone who can troubleshoot for me when something goes wrong with the Wi-Fi, too. Who do you use?"

Let your parent see that you are respectfully asking their opinion and acknowledging their experience. Practically speaking, it will also help you understand who's already doing what for them, and if those existing services are working out or not.

If you live nowhere near your parent (like me), asking them to give you a housekeeping recommendation is not going to be useful. In that case, open up a conversation about what their local friends do. But if you do live close by, maybe you and your parent can even split the cost of services like a cleaner, grocery delivery, or a dog walker.

If the personal referrals don't work out, offer to find some options and let your parent have some control by interviewing or checking online references.

THE "FOOT IN THE DOOR" APPROACH

If your parent already has someone helping them a bit, see if that helper will provide additional services. Will the guy who cuts your parent's lawn also shovel snow and trim the hedges? Sometimes these extra bits may be listed in the job description, and other times the service provider will add them in to build on an existing relationship.

Bringing this up could sound like this:

"Hey, Mom—you've got someone who takes care of your yard when you go to the lake house, right? I wonder if he might be interested in a little more regular work, since he could probably use the business. Maybe he could help with some of the heavy stuff this fall, like putting the garden to bed and hauling off the leaves."

As another example, if your parent is currently getting assistance with cleaning, you could bring up how much easier that makes their living situation as a bridge to another topic that could help them even more, such as suggesting the delivery of one or two meals per week. Getting some ready-to-eat food in smaller portions into their fridge can be a good way to ease into the idea of not always making everything themselves.

You may need to take things step by step until your parent is comfortable accepting help. Maybe you could suggest someone who will "help with the heavy stuff" while your parent works alongside them. The "extra set of hands and a sturdy back" approach is often a good one, building up trust and making sure that the person hired does it the way that your parent prefers.

Overcoming the "I don't want to be a burden on you" narrative

Whether this phrase is used with sincerity, or as one of the greatest hits of a guilt trip, it stabs you right in the heart. You're probably thinking something like, "I agree! So, let's fix this because worrying about it is the actual burden!"

It can help to turn things upside down. Does Bob the lawn-care guy need the job to help pay for his kids' tuition? Your mom is helping *him*. Does Rowan need the work experience to get into her trade school program? Setting up your mom's computer helps *her*. Does Palvir need the volunteer hours to graduate high school? Good—mutual benefit.

If you're lucky enough to have a housekeeper and you live close by, you can always try this:

> "I use this cleaner, but I just don't have enough work for her. Could she come to your house on Mondays so I can keep her? It would be a perfect solution for me and for her."

THE "I JUST CAN'T HELP YOU DO EVERYTHING" APPROACH

Families are complex—they have birth order, cultural norms, gender roles, and more woven through them. This is especially true when care comes from relatives, as some parents believe that their children or extended family should move in with them, or take them in, or do dutiful things around the parent's house.

In fact, that's mostly what ends up happening: Caregivers of older adults report spending an average of twenty to twenty-five hours per week on free care—and this is an underestimation.[1]

But there can come a point when even with these norms, cultural expectations don't match up with the realities of your life, and you just don't have twenty-plus hours to spare.

Bringing up this tricky issue could sound like this:

"Grandpa, I know you'd like me to be here most days so I can fix things around the house or take you places. I get it and I care about you, but I just can't. I've got some options we can think about instead. Besides, we'd end up butting heads and I'd rather we have a good relationship where we play golf together instead of a bad relationship where we argue in your workshop trying to fix the dresser drawers."

It could also sound like this:

"Mom, just because I'm single and my brothers and sisters have kids, that doesn't mean I'm some kind of spinster who can move home and devote all my time to you and the house. It just can't work. My job is important to me and it's in a different city. I own my apartment and I need to take care of it. I'd love to talk to you about coming over every Saturday, but let's find some help for the days in between."

THE "SHOCK AND AWE" APPROACH

The goal here is presenting your parent with some extremely compelling evidence that if they don't get help now, they're going to have to move out of the family home and into assisted living or long-term care.

Tread carefully here. You might consider a modified version of this where you weave into your conversation how you saw "on the news" that one of the key reasons that seniors have to go into long-term care is because they don't have help at home.[2] Emphasize how in the case of a health crisis like a fall that causes a broken hip, it can quickly become too late to put home support into place.

But if you need to bypass gentler strategies and lay down the law as a reality check, be prepared for fallout. It may be what needs to be done, but it can be emotionally challenging for everyone. Save this approach for when you really need it.

3

How can I work with family members to coordinate my parent's care?

Let's set some expectations at the very beginning: People don't change much, even when it comes to everyday or emergency care for your aging parent. If your macho brother was always too busy to help around the house, chances are he's not going to be volunteering to scrub your mom's kitchen every day. If your left-at-seventeen-and-never-looked-back sister hated your hometown and moved to France, she probably won't want to return to the ol' homestead in her middle years and take your dad to the doctor.

Some folks may surprise you, though, so starting off by including everyone in this conversation can really help. I've seen more than one estranged adult child decide that they have a duty to lend a hand, much to everyone else's open-mouthed astonishment. I've also seen scenarios where siblings who had little to do with each other for decades actually come together and reconnect around common parental caregiving duties. So, hope springs eternal!

I'm going to refer to your parent's helpful unpaid care team as the "siblings." But of course, they may not be your siblings: They could be friends, family-of-choice, other relatives, in-laws, volunteers from a faith or cultural community, or even your parent's significant other.

Signs it's time to have the conversation

Here are the three most common triggers for this type of discussion.

***Your parent is starting to have trouble managing on their
own, but they've never had the kids help out in any real
way.*** You might have popped by and seen that things are
looking, and smelling, a bit funky. Your mom is getting a bit
wobbly on her feet, or your dad really shouldn't be dragging the
garbage bins to the curb anymore.

In this situation, you might get your siblings ready for the big
conversation by saying something like this:

> "Mom has hit that stage of life where she needs some help. I
> know things have been going well without us so far, but now,
> I think we need to sit down and figure out how we're going
> to lean in a bit and divvy up some tasks. If you can, visit her
> before our meeting, have a look around the house, and talk
> to her about what's getting hard and what she'd like a hand
> with. Then, let's set up a time to talk about our observations
> and make a bit of a plan, even an informal one."

Well, that's the ideal form. However you actually word it, try
to avoid sounding like, "Hey losers, get your heads out of the sand
and for the love of all that's holy try to be useful for a change." I
mean, you might not be wrong, but those are *inside* voice thoughts.

***Your parent is dealing with a new acute health issue, like
an illness or a fall.*** Don't assume that rushing to help on day
one of an emergency episode is all there is to supporting your
parent. In the moment, your parent might even wave away your
offers of assistance (unless they're the high-needs type and like
the attention).

But the reality is that healing, and help, will come in stages.
Assume that the first few days will require intense, around-
the-clock care. After the first week, there will still be follow-up
appointments to drive your parent to, prescriptions to pick up,
and maybe even the joys of helping with bathing and toileting.
A few weeks later, it might be sorting through bills and pitching
in with the housekeeping. Recovery takes longer than you think,
so making a plan with your family members that covers up to
six months is the most realistic.

One sibling feels like they're "doing everything." Whether or not this is actually true, the fact that one sibling is feeling put upon, overwhelmed, taken advantage of, or exhausted is enough to prompt a broader sibling meeting. This may require everyone to use their best manners, express their appreciation, and in some cases, bite their tongues. After your sibling's feelings have been soothed, your goal will be resetting the narrative around the current situation by figuring out what everyone can do to make the work more equal from now on.

Preparing for the conversation

I recommend sitting down ahead of time and brainstorming your answers to some of these questions. But don't go in with a full plan, unless you've been asked to take the Head Planner role, and even then, proceed with caution. We all know folks who have the "you can't tell me what to do" gene (my husband has a full helping). It doesn't necessarily mean that they're stubborn, but it does mean you need to approach them in a spirit of inquiry and curiosity rather than handing them a list and saying, "do this." A few folks do like receiving the to-do list, but they're few and far between. You know the siblings you're working with best.

Category	Questions
Personalities	• Which sibling likes to take the lead in family discussions? How can you prompt them to step back sometimes? • Which likes to stay quiet or disengaged? How can you prompt them to contribute? • Do any siblings require you to walk on eggshells as they may blow up if they don't get their way? How can you reduce the chances of a major conflict?

Group dynamics	• Is there a sibling who has more influence with your parent than any of the others? (Think "Mom always loved them best.") • Which siblings get along, and which ones don't? • Is there an estranged or "outsider" sibling who needs to be pulled back in? • Is there any existing resentment between siblings or from sibling to parent? (Think "Dad paid for Kevin's college tuition but not Denise's, and Denise hasn't forgotten it.")
Skills	• Do any of the siblings have backgrounds in relevant areas like finance, law, health care, or social work? • Is anyone particularly good with the in-person, day-to-day work that can often be invisible? (Like keeping your parent's house clean or bringing over home-cooked meals.) • What do each of the siblings absolutely hate? (Like doing taxes or cleaning out a bedpan.)
Distance and transportation	• Who lives nearby and who lives far away? • Out of the siblings who live nearby, who would you designate as the "emergency contact"? • How can the far-away siblings support the nearby ones? • Who can drive? How does everyone prefer to travel? • Do any of the siblings have work or family obligations that require them to be away on trips a lot?
Existing obligations	• Are any of the siblings already managing physical or mental health situations of their own? • Does anyone already have caregiving responsibilities? (Such as for children or aging in-laws.) • How flexible is each sibling's workplace when it comes to caregiving leave? • Is anyone not working a traditional full-time job? Do they have more time to spare than others?
Money	• Does your parent have enough money for their expenses, or will siblings have to pitch in? • Is there a pot of family funds that siblings could use to pay for caregiving expenses? (Like car mileage and parking or flights home.) • Are there richer and poorer siblings? Should everyone have to contribute an equal amount, or should each pay according to their resources? • What government programs exist for caregiver benefits or tax relief in each sibling's jurisdiction? (Check to see whether each sibling can claim these benefits individually, or whether only one person is allowed to claim them.)

Strategies for having the conversation

Depending on your parent's mental and physical capacity, figuring out everyone's duties could be as simple as deciding who drives your great-aunt to bingo every week or as difficult as coming up with an around-the-clock caregiving schedule. To learn more about mental capacity specifically and how it affects the kinds of decisions you and your siblings will need to make, check out chapter 8 as well as the chapters on powers of attorney starting on page 95.

Regardless of your family's situation, here's my quick list of tips for managing a family meeting.

Set expectations for arrival: Ask everyone to show up about fifteen to forty-five minutes before you plan to start discussing the real business. This helps create a more relaxed mood and stops people from getting irritated at the sibling who's "always late."

Here's a good way to lay out the schedule.

> "We're starting off casually. I'm thinking food, drinks, and catching up from 6:00 to 6:30 PM. The real talking should begin at about 6:30 to 7:00."

Reconnect and snack: Set out a table of nibbles (something light—now isn't the time for a full sit-down dinner). Let people chat and reestablish that you're all real people who generally care about each other (or a reasonable facsimile thereof). Ask after your siblings' kids, their dogs, their golf game, their kitchen renovation, whatever.

Signal the transition: Before shifting to business, clean up and grab coffee, tea, or any other drinks folks need. (Except alcohol, if at all possible! You need clear heads for communication.) Have some pens or paper in case people want to take notes. If you're fancy enough to have a written agenda (and you know this won't intimidate your siblings by making things feel too formal), hand out copies. Otherwise, verbally outline the areas you'll be reviewing together.

Acknowledge emotions: Then, begin by sharing how you're feeling. It can sound something like this:

> "Thanks so much for coming today, everyone. Before we start on the real stuff, I want to check in and see how everyone is feeling. I'm not sure if I'm alone here, but I'm feeling really unsettled and worried. Anyone else on the same page? Or do people have some different emotions going on?"

If your family is okay with a more structured opening, consider doing a round of "three words and you're in." Like the name suggests, you say three words to describe your emotions and end with "I'm in" to signal that you're now focused on this task together. It sounds like this:

> "I feel overwhelmed, connected, and happy. And I'm in."

> "I feel sad, anxious, and worried. And I'm in."

> "I feel excited and also worried, but upbeat. And I'm in."

These emotion-acknowledgement exercises can really create a wonderful sense of connection. At the same time, I can't imagine saying something like this to my brother, who would look at me like I've asked him to share his opinion on the role of taxidermy in modern decorating. Then he'd say something like, "I feel like you're an idiot. Let's start this stupid meeting." (And being the smarty-pants younger sibling, I'd probably correct him by saying, "That's not a real emotion—you aren't doing it right.") But if you can, try to express at least some feelings in whatever way that's natural for your family.

Be gentle: Remember that these people are your family members, not your work colleagues. They have emotions about what's happening to your parent and may feel caught up in hidden (or not-so-hidden) old family resentments, so choose your words carefully.

As always, use "I" statements (like "I feel worried" or "I am overwhelmed") and talk about yourself more than others as much as possible. Be curious rather than critical. (For example, you might say, "I'm curious about how we can make sure everyone feels up-to-date and involved" or "I'm interested to know if any of you are also experiencing extra costs.")

Save the realest stuff for later: Once the meeting is over, arrange a meeting to talk with someone to who isn't in your family and won't be involved in these discussions. You could schedule a therapy appointment or find a good friend for a full-on verbal dump session. That way, it'll be easier to ensure that frustrations and emotional explosions don't make it into your carefully managed family meetings. And don't forget to smile! (No, not like that. Without the scary teeth. . . . You'll do great.)

Beyond those general best practices, here are some specific items you'll likely want to cover.

TALK MONEY

Money is hard, I know. But the amount you have access to affects every other topic on this list, so why not get it out of the way first? To make the process less painful, there are terrific resources on budgeting and financial literacy available online. If your parent has a lawyer or financial advisor, now's a great time to make an appointment and go over how the finances stand and what the likely future costs might be.

If your parent can already afford the care they need, then why are you even reading this chapter? (Just kidding—there's still stuff to discuss.) If they can't, then research benefits and government help. After that, you and your siblings will be covering some of the costs, which is where the question about dividing bills evenly or splitting them based on some other method comes in.

OUTSOURCE AND AUTOMATE

In the previous chapter, we talked about different kinds of help around the house that your parent can hire. Revisit the checklist on page 19 to see what tasks you can pay other people to take off your and your siblings' plates.

And don't forget the potential for automation in our "there's an app for that" world. For example, beyond Meals on Wheels, there are all kinds of food delivery options to explore for folks who live in urban or suburban areas. Also, if your parent (or one of the siblings) doesn't drive and taxis are hard to come by, they can try ride-sharing apps—you can even set up onetime or recurring rides for someone else from anywhere in the world.

There are also many apps that help caregivers stay in contact with each other and keep track of which tasks have been done. On your parent's phone, you can even set up apps reminding them to take medication, eat, or to check their blood pressure. (Just be aware that a blizzard of reminders becomes easy to ignore. Choose carefully.)

Additionally, if your parent hasn't already done this, you can move bill payments and check deposits online. In some cases, a joint account for household expenses can be a practical tool.

DON'T OVERLOAD THE NEARBY SIBLING

It can be easy to leave the bulk of the family caregiving to the (often female) sibling who still lives close to your parent. But just because she's geographically convenient doesn't mean she wants or should have to do everything—she needs holidays, too!

If you have a sibling who's already in this situation, make the issue front and center during the family conversation. Ask them how many hours per week they spend on caregiving and create a list of all the jobs they're currently doing. Then, set a goal of how many hours they should realistically be working and redistribute their jobs until they reach that goal.

BRING IN THE "NO HELP" SIBLING

At the other end of the spectrum, often there's a sibling who doesn't want to help out—or is just plain bad at it. If there's a question of elder abuse, then of course, this sibling shouldn't have any responsibility for your parent. But otherwise, they need to pitch in so that resentment and other nasty feelings don't put any relationships in danger.

During your meeting, everyone should be realistic about whether one of these "no helpers" exists in your group. In a "pre-meeting" that doesn't include this sibling, map out what the caregiving duties would look like with zero help from them. Then, envision a more optimistic situation by figuring out if there's anything they likely *can* do. (For example, they might provide tech support once a month or set up ride-sharing from a distance, if remote tasks are better for them than in-person ones.)

Another way to approach this is by assigning a monetary value to each of the responsibilities you'd like this sibling to take on. Then, you can give them the choice of either providing help themselves or paying for someone else to perform the duties.

SET UP A SCHEDULE (WITH BREAKS!)

An online shared calendar is terrific for blocking out exactly when each sibling is available, either for performing a specific task or being the "on call" person who's in charge of saving the day in an emergency. Everyone's vacations or other "off duty" times should also be clearly listed. And really commit to updating this schedule, even as people's life situations or the level of home care change.

MAKE AN EMERGENCY PLAN

No matter how perfect your master "sibling schedule" turns out, at some point, your parent is going to need extra care. Maybe your dad had a fall and needs help as he recovers, or your step-mom finally had her cataract surgery and needs someone to be her extra set of eyes for a couple of weeks.

Ideally, you should have a strategy in place way before any unexpected events roll around. This can look pretty similar to your everyday plan but can involve elements like who can take time off work, whose work has paid or unpaid caregiving leave, and who can afford to buy a plane ticket at the last minute. This is when having a smooth communication system (like those caregiver connection apps I mentioned) is key.

CHECK IN REGULARLY

Like any good plan, your strategy will need to be reviewed and updated as things change and when new information comes along. Even if nothing is going wrong, setting up meetings four times a year is a good goal.

During check-ins, you can update cost estimates, go over health care status reports, and identify issues that could come up in the near future. Also, bring up any changes to your family situation (can your niece who just had a baby no longer act as the on-call person for emergencies?) and make sure that communication systems are working for everyone.

As much as it can be a hassle to herd siblings and create a workable strategy together, you may be surprised by how much better you feel once the plan is in place and your mental tally of "what ifs" is shortened. Anything that saves you from late-night sessions staring at the ceiling and wondering if your parent is getting the help they need is worth a lot!

4

Does my parent need to downsize their possessions?

Imagine if someone casually rolled into your house and said, "We're going to get rid of half your stuff!" There'd be tears, raised voices, and irrational attachment to a collection of beach shells you have gathered over the course of twenty years of vacations. So, when the decision has been made that your parent is moving somewhere new and needs to downsize, first you should take a deep cleansing breath and do some warm-up stretches. Yes, it's going to require physical and logistical work—when people talk about "emotional labor," this is what they mean, especially if you're trying to avoid battles and hurt feelings.

Why is this so hard? Because we *are* our stuff. Not to get materialistic, but in so many ways, the things we accumulate around us are how we mark our accomplishments, anchor our memories, and measure the passage of time.

But don't fear! This chapter will help you keep your head while getting rid of the couch. It provides practical guidance on the essentials to think about when downsizing, how to support your parent through some very difficult choices, and how to honor their lifestyle and couch-style without getting into a fight about it—and without your parent feeling like the things they've treasured aren't valued.

Signs it's time to have the conversation

This one is easy: Is your parent moving out of their current living space, whether they're headed to a smaller apartment or into long-term care? Then it's time. But even if they're staying put, this chapter may be useful to you.

Sometimes, it's not so much downsizing but *decluttering*. Related to the chapter on age-proofing the home (page 7), your parent may not need to move if they can get rid of things and reorient how they're using space in their house. This is a considerably less momentous job and can be done slowly over time—but watch out, as it will be postponed time and time again without the deadline of a move.

Or it could be *decamping*. Your mom might need to live on the main floor, since she can't manage stairs anymore. Maybe she's rearranging her home so a caregiver can move in. Sometimes decamping can be almost as much work, particularly if you're going to renovate the original home to make it more age-friendly.

Finally, it could be an unexpected *upsize*. Sometimes your parent may want a different shape of house or a more rural lifestyle; they might trade the smaller "up and down" of a townhouse and the value of a city property for a bigger ranch-style home outside an urban center. In this case, they could actually buy more furniture and have more room for storage, plus extra bedrooms and bunk beds ready for visits from the grandkids. In this case, some of the tips here might still help you lend them a hand with reshuffling everything.

Preparing for the conversation

Before we get to the strategies, one piece of guidance: Do. Not. Judge.

This is your parent's stuff, their taste, their *life* reflected in objects—not yours. And while they *might* hate that peach floral vase as much as you do and feel fine about chucking it out, they might actually love it. Or they loved the person who gave it to them. Or it was a gift, and they feel an obligation to keep it. You can never tell, so get ready for them to hold on to a truly peculiar macaroni-encrusted sparkly piece of Father's Day "artwork" like it's the Crown Jewels.

To avoid upsetting the delicate balance by assuming one way or another, before you begin, practice a pleasant "straight face" expression. Imagine you're being asked, "Isn't my new baby the most beautiful ever?" over and over again or, "Does this outfit make me look fat?" Warm and supportive murmurs (or outright lies if absolutely necessary) can keep the temperature down.

Strategies for having the conversation

ADDRESS THE EMOTIONAL JOURNEY BEFORE YOU TALK LOGISTICS

Sit down with your parent to understand their expectations and goals. You might call it getting your parent's buy-in for your genius moving plan, or you might consider it a walk down memory lane—but, however you understand it, I promise it's important to work on resolving the emotional impact before you call the charity shop or figure out who gets the silverware.

Try to cover all of the following things in one or more pre-meetings. Do it gently with a warm level of care and inquiry if you can—and if not, fake it. You're here to ask open-ended questions and provide prompts that help them work through the transition and honor their past in the family home. (Think Oprah or Marie Kondo.)

What are they trying to achieve?

Figuring out broad goals can help you come up with the right kind of downsizing plan from the very beginning—preventing you from realizing halfway through your aunt's move into her new condo that she wants a suburban house's worth of potted plants to come with her.

Here are some ideas on how to guide those conversations.

> "Mom, I'm really hoping I can help with your move, and first I want to understand what's important to you. I know we're going to downsize. But is the goal to take the existing things you have and move whatever you can into the new place? Or do you want to start fresh with new furniture and decorations?"

"Dad, close your eyes and envision what the new place would ideally look like. Do you want your library there, or are you more into ebooks now? Do you still want that sports memorabilia wall, or is that something you'd like to give away? What's most important to you in a new home?"

How do they feel about downsizing?

Are they anxious? Excited? Overwhelmed? Resentful? You may need to redirect this part of the conversation away from measurements and square footage several times. Be open and curious, and use "I" statements if you can.

"How does this feel for you? What are you looking forward to—clearing out the clutter? What are you worried about—fitting the furniture you love into the smaller space?"

"When I first moved to a smaller apartment in the city, I was excited for a fresh new look, but I was also emotional about leaving behind some family heirlooms. I was worried and a bit overwhelmed by going through all my clothes and having to jam my wardrobe into such small closets. I had really mixed feelings. It was satisfying to weed out my clothes but letting go of some of those things hurt—I'd rather have kept them. What about you?"

When was the last time they moved?

For some people, moving is a great adventure, especially if they've been moving into increasingly larger places. For others, the idea is about as appealing as a month-long root canal. Ask your parent to reminisce about the last time they moved. It can help get them into a more adventurous spirit and remind them that change can be good, too.

Q: "When was the last time you guys moved?"

A: "Oh, well let me see. I guess your father and I moved into this house in 1975, and we've been here ever since."

Q: "How did you find this place? What made you buy it?"

A: "We drove past this house one day, and an older woman was hammering a sign into the front yard. Your father just about jumped out of the car and ran up to her, sweet-talking his way into a tour. We gave the owner our last five dollars and a note that said we had a legal option and that we'd buy the house. Can you imagine?"

(Okay—Mom and Dad, this is the one part that is a little bit about you. But even though I borrowed your great story about how you bought your first and only house, I promise the rest of the book is absolutely *not* about you.)

Q: "Where were you living before that?"

A: "An apartment down on Main Street. Actually, it was a great little apartment. Close to all the shops and the museums. We could walk to everything, and we saw more friends there than when we moved out here to the suburbs."

And there's your opening. If you pick up on these types of cues, you can get them thinking about the advantages of the new place—for example, maybe it's more centrally located, or closer to vibrant shops and museums. Pounce on it!

Consider the context: Is it loss, excitement, or both?
One of the key reasons people downsize is, frankly, because they have to. They may not be able to manage the stairs safely anymore, or they might need a unit that doesn't require as much outdoor upkeep. Think about what's precipitating your parent's move and dig into that a bit so you can keep those hidden emotions from permeating during the actual downsizing, which will already be overwhelming enough.

"Mom, can you tell me about how you feel moving after losing Harry?"

"Dad, I know this move is really to support Mom's dementia. How are *you* feeling about moving to this place?"

How much time do they have?

This can be about managing everyone's expectations, and it can be quite revealing. Don't just ask how long they have until their move—find out what kind of flex time there might be around that.

> "Cheryl, you and Mom have a three-bedroom house and you're moving to a seniors' condo, which is about a quarter of the size. I was wondering how long there is before the move-in time, and if there can be some crossover. Can you maybe leave the house a month after you get the new apartment so you can move things over more slowly? Or are you planning to do the moves out and in at the same time?"

> "Dad, I'm really happy to help with your move. I have two weekends where I can come up with the kids to help, but the whole job will probably take longer than that. Do you have a plan for a timeline?"

How can you be most helpful?

This is great to ask upfront because it may not match your expectations. The goal is to give your parent a sense of control, so they don't feel overwhelmed, resentful, or as though you and the extended family have shown up to toss out their whole life overnight. Even if a big purge needs to happen, get them to agree on who should do what beforehand—it helps.

> "Mom, what can I do that would be the most helpful? Dan and the teenagers are willing to lend a hand, too. Where do you think they would be most useful?"

Who's the best person to help?

If things start to get hairy, you might need to ask this tough question and be ready to hear "Not you." Even if you feel obligated to take charge, your parent might prefer to go through their stuff with a friend, a grandchild, an acquaintance, or even a professional. (Yes, there are people you can pay to do this with your parent. It may be cheaper than therapy—just sayin'.)

"Tony, I'm happy to help, but I was wondering if your daughter might like to do this part with you. Most of the things in your house are from before you married our mom, so it might be important to her. Just let me know either way."

"Uncle Raza, you brought over so many lovely things from the old country. I'm worried they might not find good homes if we donate them to a regular charity. Should we call the cultural center to see if someone can go through the house with you and make sure these things go to folks who can appreciate them?"

AGREE ON THE TYPE OF DOWNSIZE

Knowing how dramatic the downsize will be can help set expectations. It may be possible to transfer the entire contents of certain rooms, while in others, nothing will make the cut. If you can physically be there (or get carried around on FaceTime), go through each room of your parent's new home and make lists of what they would like to have with them.

You can also ask if they'd like a completely fresh start in which they take the minimum and totally redecorate the new place. This is especially likely if they're either moving somewhere with a completely different style or traveling a great distance that makes it cheaper to buy new furniture than to ship the old.

Strategies for taking action

GATHER YOUR TOOLS

Grab the following helpful items.

- A floor plan of your parent's new space with measurements (if possible)
- Measuring tape
- The "No Questions" box
- Your phone (for taking pictures)
- Boxes and bags for storage

- Papers with the labels "Absolutely Keep," "Maybe Keep," "Storage," "Give Away," and "Trash"
- Moving wrap or ropes
- Colored markers or labels
- A sense of humor
- Planned breaks from each other
- Snacks and rewards

The "No Questions" box

Designate a box that will contain things your parent wants to keep no matter what—no arguments, no justifications. Base the size of the box on the size of the space they'll be moving into. This helps to orient them to its size and scale ("Sorry, the stuffed marlin isn't going to fit in there") and reinforces a feeling of control for them. You always thought that ceramic frog was hideous? Tough cookies—they love it and it's going in the box!

START WITH THINGS THEY DON'T CARE ABOUT

Begin somewhere that's already tidy and small, like the laundry room or linen closet. These are also generally practical, unemotional spaces.

Leave the big or cluttered areas like attics, storage spaces, garages, and kitchens for later. If you're like me, just thinking about tackling those makes me want to a) give up, b) throw up, c) go to a movie, or d) consider the merits of an insurance fire. Most of those places are cluttered because they're filled with things that are hard to get rid of. Once you've built up some momentum, you can come back to these "home storage limbo" locations.

GET RID OF THE BIG STUFF

Try to realistically understand your parent's needs. If they're moving into a two-bedroom house, they probably need just the two beds, and getting rid of any others frees up a lot of space. If they're moving to a place that doesn't have room for more than six people at the table, toss the extra chairs first. If the large sectional sofa won't fit, get that out the door early on. Giant coffee table? Out. Enormous floor lamps? Bye!

The exceptions are big pieces of furniture that hold many precious things, like a china cabinet. Keep those where they are until you have a place where the smaller items can be safely stored or given away.

EMPTY OUT THE ROOMS THEY WON'T HAVE IN THEIR NEW PLACE

Bedrooms: Does their old home have four bedrooms, but their new unit has just one? Clear out the extra bedrooms.

Dining room: Does your parent have a full-size formal dining room with a table and chairs for twelve in their current home but only a breakfast bar in their new place? Get rid of the dining room furniture.

Living room: In a downsize, some of these gathering spaces will significantly shrink or disappear altogether. If they want to bring some living room furniture, identify what fits into the new space, then get rid of the rest.

Home office: Your parent probably won't need that giant mahogany desk, big desk chair, floor-to-ceiling bookshelf, and matching file cabinets. See if anything could be reused in a small workspace and part with the rest.

Home gym: Time to start eyeing this equipment for resale. Keep a few weights, the yoga mat, or whatever else seems portable, but the rest can go.

Hobby space: Think workshop, craft room, or indoor greenhouse. Tread carefully while emptying these rooms, since this can be hard for many people—not just because they're usually filled to the brim, but because they're full of passion projects. They also often involve identity (a capable handyperson, a superb seamstress, or a creative gardener), which can lead to a real sense of loss. Figure out a meaningful way to pass on these cherished items and see if it's possible to keep some tools, crafts, or plants.

These items can often find meaningful homes even if there isn't a relative who wants them. Does your parent's new place have a gardening club? Many cities have tool library programs. And there's a rising movement of "Men's Sheds" clubs that allow older men to gather and work on projects together.

Then have a break. Because wow, that's a lot, emotionally and physically.

PACK THE THINGS THEY WANT TO KEEP

Now it's time to identify the things your parent really wants to keep. These may be figurines, framed pictures, a couple of lamps, certain books, or your mother's extensive jewelry and shoe collections. . . . Empty a designated room, then pack up these things and store them there.

HANDLE THE RANDOM EXTRA STUFF

Kitchen duplicates

I'm the worst at this. If I have one spatula, surely two is better (or in my case, six). Same with things like cutting boards, trays, bakeware, and glassware. But then again, I often entertain for gatherings of twenty-five or more. It's unlikely that your parent will be hosting on such a large scale in their new place, and their big kitchen may be shrinking to a small kitchenette.

Be careful here: Getting rid of that extra tableware isn't just about your mom's unwavering desire to own twelve casserole dishes, but also about memories of hosting big family and social events. Tossing out those duplicate kitchen items may feel to her like a future of being less useful. Be gentle and make sure to talk about how those traditions and events will still continue even with her fulfilling a new role.

Crafts and games

You may have a strong desire to tell your mother to finally give up on the crafts she's never finished. But crafting is also a great solo or group activity that keeps fingers nimble, eyes sharp, and creative juices flowing. So, instead of grabbing all the wool, fabric, glue guns, and wreath forms and tossing them to the curb, try to pare them down into a portable collection. Consider buying a portable organizer or rolling crafting cart that can close up and be stored in a closet or in the corner of a room. Donate your parent's extra crafting supplies to schools, women's shelters, seniors' homes, or to others in your circle.

Puzzles are bulky and seem to sit on a shelf forever after they've been completed. Ask which ones your parent wants to keep, paying attention to those which have big enough pieces for aging hands and eyes to manage. You may want to donate the rest to the communal space of your parent's new home or start a "puzzle library" trading system with friends and family. The same applies to board games.

Collections

Collections can be tricky, emotional, and laden with immeasurable value. You will likely need to work with your parent on this one.

Are there a few things that can be preserved, or a way to subdivide the collection? For example, all the Royal Doulton figurines they got for their wedding will stay, but the ones given by a friend will be donated to charity. Maybe there's a way of presenting your parent's collection—things that were spread all over the house could be put into a shadow box and mounted on the wall. Or perhaps take a photo of the collection and blow it up into a lovely, framed picture. It could be an opportunity to inspire grandchildren to collect by giving each of them a few of your parent's items. (Except not those weird tourist teaspoons. What are they even for, anyway?)

MISCELLANEOUS TIPS AND TRICKS

If you get stuck on any of the steps above, try out some of these solutions.

Be practical about what takes up space

I once found myself in the middle of an intense discussion with a friend's grandmother. She was groaning about downsizing and was tearing her beating heart out about having to get rid of her collection . . . of *thimbles*. She had a lot of them—about thirty. But while she was agonizing about whether to keep her collection, she never considered that the question was a non-issue because it fit in a single Ziplock!

Thimbles are not the hill to die on because they pass the volume and mass test. But no one was talking about the grand piano in the living room, which definitely fails the test. So, make sure to be realistic about what size objects really need close attention.

Rent storage

A dear friend of mine has a wonderful father in his nineties. They have comfortable family money, and her father just sold the large family home in the big city before moving into a fully furnished small bungalow in a teeny rural community with a view of the ocean and his loving kids close by.

Sounds perfect, but . . . "Where is the *stuff*?" I asked her one day. He was a collector who kept every receipt, book, and file he ever had.

"He wants to go through it all personally," she said. I cocked my head, looking at her inquiringly.

She smiled broadly. "Storage," she said. "He can afford it. He wants to keep it. He wants to go through it someday. Okay."

Storage. Genius. Sometimes it saves the fight, your parent's dignity, and your sanity, too.

Get them into the mercantile spirit

With online sites like Craigslist, Facebook Marketplace, Kijiji, and more, your parent may be astounded by how quickly their "vintage" stuff sells. Remember, marketing is everything: Take good-quality photos with decent lighting to provide all relevant details. Maybe give this job to a tech-savvy grandchild who wants to help but doesn't know what to do. Your parent might think this is a fantastic idea and start rubbing their hands together at the prospect of ready cash for their stuff. If nothing else, it's good for the environment and can help offset the cost of moving.

Give the legacy gifts
Instead of leaving specific items to family and friends after their death, your parent might consider giving them away now, in life. This allows your parent to see that their items are being used and valued.

Hire help
If you or your parent is really not looking forward to this whole process, consider hiring a professional. There are associations of "senior movers" and "downsizing experts," and geriatric care professionals can usually recommend some people, too. You can sometimes write this expense off on your parent's taxes—research the rules in your area.

Don't be a jerk—this is hard
Let's be clear: At the end of the day, your opinions aren't the driving force because this isn't about you. And no matter how many times your mom tells you that if only you were here in person to help, she would start the downsizing process immediately, calling her bluff may not be the way.

Think of the many, many times you've thought of other, better things to do than going through all your possessions, tossing out things you care about, and then cleaning, packing, and scrubbing. And remember to be nice. Let your parent reminisce. Let it take some time if you have it. Maybe bring a grandchild into the mix—often, a grandparent will feel less defensive around children, and kids can bring a great deal more humor to the situation.

Is it time for my parent to move into independent living or a retirement home?

The need for some type of group living or residential care can sneak up on you and your parent. You might gradually notice signs that your parent isn't taking care of themselves—like wearing the same clothes every day. Or the change can happen suddenly—like a bad fall taking away their mobility at home.

Regardless, the idea of "going to a home" can really throw someone into an emotional spin. Some older adults see it as the beginning of the end or a sign that their children don't want to take care of them anymore. But the truth is, it can be both a huge relief for you as a caregiver and a step up in the quality of life for your parent.

Signs it's time to have the conversation

There are all kinds of red flags that can suggest your parent needs to move out of the home they know into a new one with more supports. See if any of these points sound familiar.

- Your parent is lonely and rarely interacts with anyone these days.
- Friends, extended family, or neighbors are pulling you aside to talk about how they don't see your parent outside much lately, or about how they look neglected and confused lately.
- Your parent can still make their own decisions, but they need help with their medication and daily activities, and home support isn't enough anymore.

- Your parent's chronic health problems are getting even worse.

- Your parent is *literally* falling and can't get up.

- Your parent's partner just can't manage their care any longer.

What if it's even more serious—for example, what if your parent has cognitive impairment and *can't* make their own decisions, or has been in and out of the hospital with major medical issues? In that case, long-term care might be more appropriate for them, so you should check out the section starting on page 56.

Preparing for the conversation

UNDERSTAND THE TYPES OF CARE

When you first start to research seniors' congregate care, you'll probably think, "Help! Why are there so many different terms out there?" Not only does every home, center, assisted living environment, and long-term care facility seem to have a different title, those titles can also have completely different meanings depending on where you live. Rather than try to list all the variations, I'll explain the major categories.

Independent living (aka seniors' living or retirement living): This one is actually just what it sounds like—imagine a regular apartment for an independent adult, but it's designed for better accessibility, including on-call nursing or medical care. You'll need to ask whether any day-to-day support is provided in-house or if your parent has to supply their own home care.

Retirement homes (aka supportive housing or assisted living): In this more supportive environment, your parent lives independently and usually makes their own decisions, but they need some additional help with things like meal preparation, household chores, or medical care. Retirement homes can have a wide variety of services that differ from place to place, ranging from quite minimal assistance right up to what looks a lot like long-term care. "Assisted living" typically refers to the highest level of care in this category. Some retirement homes also include "memory units" for people with cognitive impairment.

Long-term care (aka nursing homes): This comes into play when your parent requires around-the-clock care because of dementia or serious medical issues. Long-term care is often part of the healthcare system and has an emphasis on complex medical needs. Typically, you don't just check your parent into a long-term care home—there may be waiting lists, required functional and medical assessments, insurance coverage questions, and care planning.

Campus of care: These locations include several of the above options on the same overall site: There may be independent living in one area, then a block of supportive housing in another, and assisted living–level support provided within some of those housing units. Ideally, your parent remains in the same unit and more care is provided as their needs increase, but usually, there's some switching of units or floors, especially for dementia care. Campuses of care are often the ideal locations for aging in place, but they can be rarer than you'd expect.

As we go through some of the different options below, keep those terms in mind. Each one represents a different stage in your parent's life.

ASSESS YOUR PARENT'S SITUATION

Before talking about alternative living options with your parent, think about how they'll likely react. Then consider their priorities so that you can emphasize those benefits at the alternative living options to potentially make their reaction more positive. Is it safety? Being with other people? Not having to make dinner all the time? Not worrying about yard work?

Also, find out if they already have friends in certain congregate care homes—it can make a huge difference for them to move into a place where they already know someone.

At the other end of the spectrum, consider what your parent will likely hate about congregate care. What are they worried about giving up? For a lot of people, it can be the lack of a private backyard or garden space. Others are worried about not being able to bring their pets, or that the social activities will be stupid and boring. You can use these ideas of your parent's likely concerns to do research and prepare arguments in advance.

BE CLEAR ABOUT THE "WHY"

Moving into congregate care is not something everyone does—in fact, it's not something even the majority of seniors do. As adult children, we want to make sure our parents are safe, socially engaged, and, frankly, not likely to break their necks on the stairs. But we can have an uphill battle unless our parent has a specific need that's not currently being met, so it's important to identify what that need is.

For instance, if your dad recently got a dementia diagnosis, but his spouse is mentally capable and quite fit, their reason to go into congregate care could be twofold: Your dad needs the help and his spouse needs a break, plus more stimulation and social engagement. Using this information, you can make sure that the places you're considering have supports for both partners.

Some notes about timelines

People often move into retirement homes in their early eighties, with average resident ages hovering around 85 depending on location.[1] The average length of stay at an assisted living residence that offers some higher levels of care is between one to two years.[2] This is because usually, by the time an older adult is willing to move out of their home, they've progressed to having more care needs. But that shorter length of time is certainly not always the case, and it is less likely at the lighter care end of the spectrum, where folks have moved in for social interaction, some health care, and food and cleaning supports.

HAVE SUGGESTIONS READY

Once you have a general idea of what level of care your parent needs, "go shopping" by visiting some independent living and retirement homes. You may or may not want to tell your parent about this before opening up the bigger conversation—in my experience, caution is usually best. It can be helpful, though, to bring a friend or other relative as a second set of eyes. An in-person search is best, but you can certainly start researching on the internet or over the phone if need be.

Try to come up with a list of three to five places—any more can be overwhelming. As you search, think about both what's a good fit for your parent now and which more intensive care options they might take advantage of in the future. The tips in chapter 6 on assessing whether a long-term care facility is the right fit for your parent can also be useful to keep in mind here.

You'll want to get answers about how soon a place could be available and what the cost breakdown looks like: How much is covered by insurance, how much is eligible for public assistance, and how much comes out of pocket? Most seniors' residences (at both lower and higher levels of care) can be quite pricey, unfortunately. Depending on finances, you might have to moderate your enthusiasm for your parent's big move and focus on what they can afford only if more care is absolutely necessary.

Strategies for having the conversation

THE "WHAT ARE YOUR FRIENDS DOING?" APPROACH

The easiest way to start the conversation with your parent is by asking where their friends are these days. If your parent is in their eighties or older, it's likely that they'll have friends in all kinds of living situations: in their own homes (with some receiving home care), in seniors' living or assisted living, and in long-term care. Finding out the details could sound like this:

"Hey, where's Mrs. Lee these days? Oh, she's at the Seniors' Lodge down the road? Huh. Is that the one with the gardens that lets animals in? Cool. Where are your other friends— any of them in places you like? Isn't Mr. Singh a snowbird who's in one of those seasonal residences in Florida all winter? You love the sun and hate the cold, too. Does he like the place he's at? We should check it out sometime, or I could phone his daughter and find out more."

See if you can arrange a visit for your parent to see their friends, whether that's a formal tour of the facility or just a meal together. Maybe come along yourself to find out more about the place. Even if your parent doesn't come away ready to move in immediately, the experience could help them narrow down what they do and don't like about congregate care, which is useful for future planning.

THE "TRY IT OUT" APPROACH

Many retirement homes have caregiver respite services that allow older adults to "check in" for a few days, weeks, or even months. It's jarring to move at all, but going for a temporary stay while leaving the family home essentially untouched can really help with adjustment to a new lifestyle. And if your parent hates it, they can just come back home. Naturally, this assumes that a test stay is an affordable option, but you may be able to sublet your parent's home to cover the costs.

You could introduce the idea like this:

"Mom, I'm so excited to travel overseas for work this winter. It's a real opportunity. But I'm worried about leaving you all alone. You've had some falls, and when the weather is bad, you're stuck in the house. How about we look at some options of places you could stay while I'm gone? Think of it like a hotel visit. If you try out the place where your friend Keiko is living, you guys could have some hilarious chats like you always used to."

THE "GUILT TRIP" APPROACH

This isn't my favorite strategy, mostly because it feels manipulative. But I know that families are messy, and I don't judge, especially since this option is actually pretty common and effective.

Bringing on the guilt sounds something like this:

> "Dad, I've been so worried about you since I moved far away. I'm especially anxious at night—you should see me at 3 AM! I'm a wreck and I can't sleep. I love you so much, and I know you're just not safe in this house. I feel like I'm going to fall apart if you stay here alone in your chair in front of your game shows all day. Please, for me—can we look at a few places together? I think there are some that you'd really like, and I'd be so happy knowing you have friends, good food, activities, and regular physio appointments for your leg. Please, Dad?"

Regardless of the initial approach you take, you're probably going to have to consider a mix of approaches, and you may end up cycling through them. In the end, there is always the "let's avoid long-term care—this is a way better alternative" narrative. It's not a pretty way in, but it's effective.

When is it time for long-term care, and how can we shop for the best option?

This may be the topic your parent wants to talk about the least and the one you have the hardest time bringing up: the nursing home, or as we'll refer to it, long-term care (LTC).

Only about 3 to 10 percent of seniors will ever live in an LTC home, although the likelihood greatly increases after the age of eighty-five.[1] However, this is still a reality for which you'll want to be prepared.

So, how do you know if your parent needs to be in LTC? And what if your parent's partner doesn't need this kind of support—can they still stay together? How much does it cost? What's the average wait time, and what are the rules for getting on a waiting list? Should your parent move to an LTC home across the country from their community, but closer to you? These are the questions you'll want to keep front and center in your mind as you shop for LTC.

Every answer has tradeoffs, and in some cases, you'll just be making the best of a bad situation full of worry and ill health. But when LTC is necessary, it's also often a real relief to have your parent safely cared for. (That doesn't mean you won't still feel some guilt, but chapter 14 can help with that.)

Signs it's time to take action

Usually the equation looks like this: problems with toileting + dementia + another high-needs health condition that often involves mobility issues. This combination can rarely be cared for at home. These further situations also typically call for LTC.

Your mom has been managing okay living alone with some home care. But she's been getting increasingly forgetful, and last week, she fell down the stairs and broke her hip. She's in the hospital right now, and they're trying to discharge her back to her house. You're not on board with this, since you live five hours away and know that she can't recover alone at home. Her house isn't set up for aging in place, and with her injury, she has no way of eating, toileting, or bathing on her own.

A series of strokes have left your dad paralyzed, and he also has a colostomy bag. He needs to be fed and requires a two-person transfer to get out of bed. Although he has very high needs, he's mentally capable. But your mom is small and frail with her own health issues, and she can't take care of your dad.

Your great uncle has severe mental health issues and COPD that requires oxygen. He lives alone in a rural community and can't move around the house independently. He's had a series of falls leading to concussions and is consistently malnourished.

In these cases, you rarely have the luxury of talking about whether the move will happen. You don't "put someone in a nursing home" or choose to go—that's more applicable to independent living and retirement homes (see chapter 5). When it comes to LTC, people very rarely move in unless they desperately need care. That means you'll be focusing on making the move happen as soon as possible, so here are some practical insights you'll want to investigate as you begin the process.

Preparing to take action

Based on where your parent lives, their eligibility for LTC might depend on a public funding process, criteria that must be met for qualification, or a waiting list. Some areas have waiting lists that are tens of thousands of people long, and in others, homes might even be actively recruiting more residents—so, you should start by figuring out what demand looks like in the place you have in mind. "Emergency" or "urgent" placements are sometimes prioritized even in places with higher demand.

In some jurisdictions, LTC is part of government health care services, which helps alleviate a good chunk of the costs. In those jurisdictions, individuals may have to pay only a set accommodation rate, plus an additional price for any extra "nice to have, but not required" services. In other areas, cost is determined by a mix of asset testing, private payments, and government program qualifications. The tradeoff is that when the government covers most of the costs, waiting lists are typically longer, while privately funded homes can often be easier to get into. In other jurisdictions, LTC is fully privately paid and there are homes that are actively trying to recruit residents (I confess, I've only ever seen this in the USA).

Finally, almost all LTC homes require assessments to ensure residents need their services. They'll likely look at your parent's level of performance on ADLs (activities of daily living, or basic self-care tasks like bathing and eating) and IADLs (instrumental activities of daily living, or more complex everyday tasks like shopping and paying bills). After those assessments, they will determine if they can take your parent as a resident or if their care needs cannot be met at home. In some places it will also determine placement on a waiting list.

Strategies for taking action

The best advice I can give you when searching for an LTC home is to ignore the paint—that is, to see beyond its fancy (or not-so-fancy) appearance. It's really all about the staff, the philosophy of care, the level of support, and the respect and choices given to residents. Much of the advice here also applies to the other forms of congregate care covered in chapter 5.

Here are some starting questions that can help you make a decision.

- Do residents look clean and tidy? Are they dressed neatly with their hair brushed?

- How does it smell? Is it fresh and clean, or is there a pervasive smell of urine and feet?

- Do the staff interact with residents naturally and warmly?

- What are the staffing levels like? You'll want to know not only how many hours of worked care are available (four hours of daily care per resident is a good starting point but it depends on the care needs of your particular parent), but also what kind of coverage there is at night or on weekends. Visit at different times to see for yourself.

- Are residents involved in activities?

- How close is the LTC home to your parent's previous community? What's the proximity to family and friends?

- What's the food like? (I can't emphasize enough how important this is.) And can residents eat what they want and with whom they want, or are they on fixed schedules?

Read on for specifics on some of these items.

PHILOSOPHY OF CARE

An LTC home's philosophy of care is a codified statement of how it strives to treat its residents. Basically, your parent's home should have one. If an LTC home doesn't clearly state which model it runs on, then it's likely to default to the institutional "medical model," which is the last thing you want.

Mind you, LTC homes almost never openly say they work on the medical model. But here is a list of clues, with the ideal LTC environment described first and the medical model second.

- Are staff wearing regular clothes, or are they in uniforms that look like scrubs?

- Do staff work in open spaces closer to residents, or do they huddle behind one main desk that's away from most interactions?

- Are residents actively engaged in building things, making food, and expressing themselves creatively, or are they left to sit in the halls?

Try to find a smaller LTC home focused on aging in place. If a home runs on a philosophy created in this century that respects residents, it will often use terms like those in the table below. (To learn more about different models of care and what makes for a great LTC experience, I recommend *Happily Ever Older: Revolutionary Approaches to Long-Term Care* by author and journalist Moira Welsh.)

Philosophies	Descriptions
Butterfly Model	Alternative
Green House Model	Emotion-focused
Montessori Model	Home-like
Nordic	Person-centered
Circle of Care	Transformative
Dementia Village	
Eden Alternative	

These alternative models of LTC were created to overcome the traditional institutional warehousing method of caring for seniors. They're all focused on improving quality of life and allowing people as much freedom and choice as possible.

They usually have a campus of care (multiple levels of congregate housing in the same location) or clusters of homes with smaller groups of people living inside. Typically, LTC homes like these have access to more staff. They also provide easy access to safe outdoor areas, plants, and sunlight, plus snacks and opportunities to be involved in meal preparation. Overall, preserving a sense of purpose in residents' days is critical to these philosophies of care, and I'm a big fan.

RESIDENTS' RIGHTS AND RESIDENT AND FAMILY COUNCILS

Ideally, the LTC home should have some kind of residents' bill of rights, whether it's determined by legislation, decided by ownership, or required by an accreditation body. You'll want to get a copy of this and read it. I'd personally get a copy of the home's overall policies and procedures, too, but I confess that may be a little overboard.

There should also be a residents' council. If your parent ends up in an LTC home with a council, encourage them to get involved. If their home doesn't have one, raise heck with the management.

Finally, there should be a family council. Here, "family" is very broadly defined—any of your parent's loved ones should be able to join, and I encourage you to do so. If your parent's LTC home doesn't have a family council, you can start one.

ROOMS

I know I said the physical environment isn't as important, but you'll still want to pay attention to your parent's future room. What is available? Are they old-style four-to-a-room wards separated only by a curtain (yuck), or are they semi-private or private? Ideally, your parent should live in a private single room with a bathroom en suite that includes bathing facilities. The last thing you want is your prim and proper mother in a shared room with mixed genders, a single toilet, and bathing facilities shared by upwards of twenty people.

If it's relevant, ask if couples can be kept together. (Or maybe your mom wants to share a room with her girlfriend—platonic or romantic.)

Also ask if you can request a certain unit or wing. Think about where the light falls during the day. If your dad's an early riser, he might want windows that face east so he can greet the sunrise. And—I can't believe this is even an issue—find out if the windows open!

FOOD AND EATING

Make sure that food is made on the premises wherever possible, since meals brought in from offsite are never as good. It's even better if residents can choose to help with food preparation. Also, check what accommodations are offered for cultural foods or religious requirements.

Many LTC residents have eating or swallowing difficulties, which can require soft foods, purees, or assistance with meals. Make sure that even these special foods are tasty and nutritious, and that the person helping with feeding is both engaging and respectful. (Your parent isn't a toddler, and we don't need a "choo-choo train!")

Sometimes LTC residents are assigned a table and time to eat. I'm not a fan of this—being forced to have lunch three hours before you're actually hungry is obnoxious, and putting a mentally active, chatty person at a table with others who are non-communicative won't be a good fit.

You should find out if residents can eat in a variety of locations, choose their meal times, and decide who to eat with. If your parent isn't a fan of breakfast, they shouldn't be required to sit around and watch everyone else have their morning toast. You can ask whether room service or all-day dining are available, too.

After taking all this into account, hopefully you're ready to find the right LTC home for your parent. But once you do, your work still isn't finished—continue to the next chapter to learn more about how to help them settle in and make the most of their new living space.

7

How can we make my parent's long-term care experience as good as possible?

Finding a long-term care home for your parent can either be an odyssey or a walk in the park if you're lucky. This chapter will guide you through making the move-in process as smooth as possible and then ensuring that your parent's stay is the best it can be. Privacy, boredom, loneliness, and adjusting to a new environment are all covered here, plus working with staff and knowing both your parent's and your rights. Overall, you'll want to figure out what kind of involvement you can (and want to!) have in long-term care life.

Moving in

BEING READY

Like I mentioned before, it's likely that your parent could get stuck on a waiting list—but once a spot opens up, you'll need to make a decision quickly. If your parent can't move in right away, they may end up back at the bottom of the list. This can obviously be super stressful, especially if you're out of town at your kid's (never-ending) baseball tournament and thus can't help with the move yourself.

PACKING SMART

If you can, pre-select the clothes, toiletries, furniture, pictures, and other memorabilia your parent wants to take and keep the necessities that will need to go right away packed up and ready. But this move likely won't happen all at once, especially if you have wiggle room to keep their home for a month or so afterward to slowly declutter and transfer things over. (See chapter 4 for help with this decluttering process.)

Label everything as you pack. If you've ever sent your kid to camp, you may remember putting peel-and-stick labels on all their clothes—you can easily purchase versions online that survive even the most powerful washing machine.

If your parent wears eyeglasses with a specific prescription, get them versions with identifiable frames to prevent them from being lost and mixed up. (Bright red or purple are always good.) Labels, glasses strings, and several backup pairs are even better.

DOING THE PAPERWORK

If your parent is mentally capable, they should be doing the mountains of paperwork themselves. But if you're acting as a substitute decision-maker, be ready with any power of attorney (POA) documents (and your pen). The LTC home will need a copy of the POA for property to set up billing, plus a copy of the POA for personal care/health care, since this decision involves your parent's health. (Confused? Just jump to the chapters about POA, starting on page 95.)

Entering LTC requires consent—contrary to jokes about sticking your mom in a home, you can't "put" someone there. Either the mentally capable (but obviously highly infirm) parent consents to become a resident or, if they're incapable of that decision, their health and personal care substitute decision-maker does so in their place.

AVOIDING THE MOVE-IN MEDICATION TRAP

I can't tell you how many times family members have told me that their parent was "temporarily" put on a calming medication—sometimes Ativan, Valium, or antipsychotics—to ease the transition into LTC. I've even seen LTC homes give them out to everyone who moves in as a matter of course. This is wrong on so many levels. Drugging someone into submission is abuse, specifically chemical abuse.

I'm absolutely not saying this happens at every facility, but you should be on the lookout for it. Medications should never be required for entry into an LTC home, and never accept these meds without doing your research and consulting a pharmacist and a health care provider. As an alternative, work with your parent to make sure they understand what's going on. When you chose a home, you made sure the staff were warm, calming, and caring, and this attitude should absolutely be present as your parent settles in.

Getting comfortable

THE ROOM

Do everything you can to make sure your parent's room is cozy and full of life. Here are some ideas.

- Set up a corkboard with family photos and label who everyone is.
- Frame interesting pictures from their childhood.
- Play the music they love.
- Keep the lights low and soft if possible.
- Decorate their door as if it's the door to their old home.
- Bring potted plants or flowers.

Some of these tips can also help you make sure that the staff know your parent's story. You'll want them to understand that your parent isn't just another patient—they're also funny and vibrant, a champion latke maker or a lover of classic cars.

MEALS

Shared meals are important for socialization and can help remind people to eat, so it's great if your parent wants to dine in the common area. But this may be too loud and overstimulating at first, so you can work with the staff to see if you and your parent can have a special dinner together instead.

It's my great hope that people of all cultures are celebrated and supported in LTC, but depending on your family's background, the food might not meet your parent's needs or desires. You can always talk to the dietary services manager to see what can be done, especially when it comes to allergies or other health issues.

THERAPY ANIMALS

You wouldn't believe how people come alive when pets are around! Some LTC homes have in-house therapy animals or scheduled visits. If not, find out if you can bring your own pet into the building or meet up with your parent outside.

ALCOHOL AND SMOKING

The LTC home can't disallow drinking, so yes, your mom is allowed her wine. Sometimes doctors' notes will include crazy things like "Mabel may have two ounces of wine once a week," but they really have no right to stipulate this. (Imagine trying to pull that in France!) The home may prefer to keep your parent's booze safely stored somewhere out of the way and that is just fine.

Of course, smoking isn't allowed inside, but LTC homes must provide a safe space that doesn't put your parent at risk of sweating or freezing to death in the elements whenever they have a cigarette.

Staying healthy

THE DOCTOR

It's a sad fact that doctors at LTC homes are often far too busy to know each resident's particular conditions and needs. Your parent is absolutely not required to become this doctor's patient, and they should keep their family doctor if possible. Or ideally, you can get your parent a proper geriatrician if possible.

THE DENTIST

Similarly, dental care in LTC is typically dreadful, so don't trust it. Sometimes LTC dentists do a partial cleaning, but they likely don't have the right equipment with them, and they almost never do restoration work. Either stick with your parent's current dentist or try to find a new one who specializes in geriatric care or accessible dentistry.

Being involved

YOUR PARENT'S RIGHTS

First and foremost, the LTC home is your parent's *home*. It's not a prison, so they have the right to leave! An LTC resident can pop over to Starbucks, go to the mall, or head to the strip club or pool hall. (Okay, I haven't seen those last two happen, but I'd cheer them on all the same.) It is, however, appropriate for your parent to be required to sign in and out for fire safety.

Even if your parent isn't mentally capable, they're still allowed to go out, although they may need some support to do so. If they're "exit seeking," try to figure out what they're looking for. Do they want some fresh air? A smoke? A nice walk down the street? There's a good chance you will get into a fight with the management about this, but you can dig out the residents' rights document for reference.

Rules about visitors can vary (and in some cases, there are absolutely no rules). Sometimes, management will implement a policy because they want families to go home, but that policy isn't actually legal. So really, you're better off reading the legislation for LTC homes in the jurisdiction where your parent lives.

Can a staff member or substitute decision-maker stop someone from visiting? Usually no, unless a visitor is actually abusing a resident or a staff member. Even if you don't want your shady cousin visiting your mom, you'll need some sort of legal reasoning beyond "he keeps asking her for money."

THE CARE CONFERENCE

Care conferences are important meetings that are supposed to involve the full interdisciplinary team supporting your parent (such as doctors, nurses, physiotherapists, administrators, personal support managers, and dietary managers), your parent (even if they aren't mentally capable of making health care decisions), you, and any other family members who want to be there. In actuality, often only a few of those professionals will attend, and they may or may not know your parent. Try to set the expectation that you want them all there in person or on a video call. However, you'll almost certainly know your parent's condition and concerns better than most of them.

These conferences typically happen on a schedule, often annually. There should be one within one to three months of the initial move to check how things are settling in. After that, you can also ask for a care conference if worries or significant changes in your parent's care needs come up. They usually take thirty to sixty minutes, and don't let yourself be rushed if you still have concerns left to address—I recommend asking for the full amount of time.

At the initial meeting, the team should work with you and your parent to come up with a written care plan. Then, you'll reference this plan at future meetings and amend it based on any new decisions.

Here are some tips for the best possible care conference.

- Ensure that the meeting is scheduled during a time of day when your parent typically feels best and when you and other interested family and friends can attend.

- If key professionals or family members can't be there, offer a hybrid meeting involving both in-person interaction and video calls.

- Email the professionals involved in your parent's care to confirm that they're coming. If someone wasn't planning on being at the meeting but you'd like to have them there, ask if they can attend.

- Bring food for the staff. They're usually run off their feet, so you can win major brownie points this way.

- If you're a substitute decision-maker (see the chapters on POA starting on page 95), exercise your right to get a copy of your parent's chart and refer to it during the meeting.

- This is a chance to ask questions about how your parent is doing, so take some time to think about what you want to know beforehand. You could ask if staff have noticed friendships, activities your parent likes, or things they *don't* like.

- Throughout the meeting, be polite and use problem-solving skills. It's unlikely that your parent will move out of this LTC home, so it's helpful to have the staff on your side.

VISIT, VISIT, VISIT

In the wake of COVID-19, LTCs have never been so short-staffed. Trained staff are often underpaid, underappreciated, and overtired, so be nice! Many of them have only minutes to do everything that needs to be done for your parent, and they are aware that this isn't ideal. Weekends, evenings, and holidays are the least staffed, so consider visiting your parent during these times. You might even be able to (informally) help cover some tasks.

Even beyond staffing concerns, visiting your parent is important. As a rule, shorter, more regular visits are better than fewer, longer ones. The reality is that most people in LTC don't get visitors, so if you have a little love left over for the other residents, an occasional chat, special treat, or hug can make someone's day.

Take the kids and the dog. Have movie nights. Bring smells and foods and other things from home. And enjoy your time as much as you can.

PART 2

Mental capacity, power of attorney, and safety

8

How do I know if my parent
has cognitive impairment
or dementia?

What probably isn't cognitive impairment: Your mom can't find her car keys. Again.

What probably is cognitive impairment: Your mom is in the driver's seat holding her car keys, but she doesn't know why she has them. She can't remember how driving works or what the keys are for.

This second category contains some pretty harrowing stuff: Getting a 3 AM call about how your dad, who lives across the country, left the house in a bathrobe twelve hours ago in the dead of winter and hasn't been seen since. Learning about your parent's weekly 3 AM calls to the local police department because of the paranoid fear that someone is breaking into their home and stealing their bananas. (I finally learned why so many older people get paranoid about disappearing bananas! According to a friend of mine who's a highly respected geriatrician, bananas are easy to fixate on because they usually live on the counter in plain sight, stand out since they're bright yellow, and can be easily counted.) There are endless versions of these stories, but they all cluster around the same things: confusion, paranoia, fear, and feeling lost.

"Losing it" in this way is our biggest fear as we age: for ourselves and for our parents. But what does it actually mean to be "losing it"? How do you know?

To answer the first question, I'll need to get into some psychology.

What are cognitive impairment and mental capacity?

Cognitive impairment is an umbrella term for anything that can affect your thinking, including all of the "big Ds": cognitive decline, dementia, depression, and delirium.[1]

Each of these have repercussions on what we call *mental capacity*. Mental capacity isn't a light switch that turns only "on" or "off" (unless you're actually in a coma). It's more like a thermostat that can be dialed up or down. (As an example: I had two kids within seventeen months. I joke that I had impaired mental capacity throughout that entire time—and I'm not completely wrong.) And it's situational—as mental capacity changes, you're usually able to make thoughtful decisions about some things but not others.

Mental capacity is, above all, *presumed*. That means you have it until proven otherwise, despite any bad choices, foolish decisions, or bizarre behavior. Because when it's proven otherwise, it's a huge deal: Declarations of incapacity functionally remove your human and civil rights.

To give you a sense of how serious it is to be declared mentally incapable, here are some examples of rights that can be taken away in that situation.

- Deciding where to live
- Choosing what to eat
- Having sex
- Getting married or divorced
- Driving
- Buying or selling anything
- Making a will
- Choosing your own doctor or caregiver
- Determining your own medical treatment

Essentially, your right to be a person and exercise basic decision-making is at risk. Because of how serious this is, we all should make the best possible effort to support someone in making decisions rather than removing their rights.

WHAT MENTAL CAPACITY IS AND ISN'T

Mental capacity is easy to explain and really hard to test. It's generally legally defined as the "ability to understand and appreciate," and inherent in this definition is the idea that someone can receive data, figure out how it applies to them and the decision they're trying to make, and appreciate what will happen as a result of their choice. The tricky part is this: They have to be *able* to understand and appreciate, but they don't actually have to do it.

Stay with me and see if this example helps.

I have three smart teenagers, with report cards and notes from teachers assuring me that this is the case. My kids know that if they leave their goalie gear, hockey sticks, gym bags, tennis rackets, backpacks, rubber boots, homework, or the entire contents of their school lockers in the front hall, I'll open the door, trip over the stuff, and get mad. They're able to understand this information and use their apparently functioning brains to decide whether they should dump their junk in the hall or put it away, and they have lots and lots of experience with this decision. I didn't give them instructions in Aramaic or make them navigate IKEA furniture assembly instructions. And yet . . .

Do they understand the information? Yes. Do they appreciate the consequences of their decisions? Yes. So, they have the *ability*—the mental capacity—to use this knowledge, but they just don't.

Let's try another scenario, this time with a parent.

Imagine your dad has diabetes, plus some kind of infection that's making his foot turn gangrenous. If he doesn't immediately get it treated, he could lose the foot or even die. He knows about doctors. He knows about medical treatments. He knows about his foot. He may even know how bad it could be if he doesn't take care of it. . . . But he doesn't. You ask him about it, and he tells you to mind your own business. His mental capacity to make the decision probably isn't at question—above all, it's presumed. He's just *not* making a decision.

Yep, I know. He has *gangrene*! And yet.

Remember, he thought it was idiotic when you got your tattoo and piercings. He probably figured you had diminished mental capacity throughout most of your teens and twenties, but he didn't have you institutionalized. Just sayin'.

I'm not really equating an eighteen-year-old's tattoo or tongue piercing with your dad's gangrenous foot. (Although he did warn you that your tongue might turn black and fall out, too, didn't he?) This is just meant to show you that bad decisions, or no decisions, do not equate with mental incapacity.

Nevertheless, you're still really worried. He might be acting confused, scared, and like he's kind of mentally losing it. You don't want to let him lose his foot, his house, or his life.

WHAT AFFECTS MENTAL CAPACITY?

Mental capacity is affected by sleep, medication, blood sugar, physical and mental health, and good ol' booze.

It can also increase or decrease over time. Some conditions improve—for instance, once babies finally decide to sleep through the night, parents get more rest and become mentally sharper. As another example, an older person might finally get diagnosed with a urinary tract infection, causing their mental confusion to dissipate once they get antibiotics and some cranberry juice.

Talking to your parent about mental capacity

Before involving a professional, you can do a DIY assessment of your parent's mental state. During this conversation, some red flags to notice are short-term memory loss, getting names and other details confused with things from their past, disorientation, and deviation from their general patterns.

- Make sure your parent can hear you, since hearing loss is astonishingly prevalent in older adults. Go to a quiet room and remove background noise like fans or air conditioning.

- Face your parent directly. If they use glasses, make sure that they're wearing the right pair.

- Check that they've eaten, are hydrated, and are as rested as possible.

- Before talking, make sure your parent is comfortable and not distracted. Are they worried about missing a package that will be delivered soon? Have they taken their medication? Do they want some tea or water? Do they need to go to the bathroom? Address anything like this first.

- Then, start to broadly discuss how they're managing in day-to-day life, keeping your face neutral and friendly. Wait, listen, and don't be afraid of pauses. Avoid asking leading questions or jumping in to fill in the response you expect.

  Try: David and I are starting to wonder how you're doing living here by yourself. How's it going?

  Avoid: I don't know how you can stand living out here all by yourself. Aren't you afraid all the time?

  Try: I wanted to check in and see what you're up to these days. What have you been doing this week?

  Avoid: Have you been sitting here all by yourself all week?

- Watch and listen for clues that your parent is covering something up. If your mom is tidily put together and has excellent social graces, she can probably fake her way through most things. Or if your dad is bluff and off-putting or warm and gregarious, he can probably manipulate the social situation to avoid revealing his own confusion. Don't fall for surface appearances—use your knowledge of your parent's typical behavior to sense if something's off, and if you do get a bad feeling, keep checking their ability to understand and appreciate.

- Try to find out if they understand their financial situation and see if you can get them to do some numerical reasoning. (But know that many seniors are very sensitive about discussing money and may tell you to butt out even if they're mentally capable.)

   Try: Hey, I had a look at your mail—I saw that your water and phone bills came in. Remind me: How much do you get from your private work pension and from the government? Let's sit down and figure out your bills. I'll grab a pen and paper if you want.

   Avoid: Tell me how much money you have in your bank account. Sit down and calculate your bills. Don't mind me. I'm just going to stand over your shoulder and see if you can still do math.

- Wherever possible, ask hypothetical "What would you do if . . ." questions to test their reasoning skills.

   Try: Hey Mom, you're out here in this rural community and storms come through a few times a year. What would you do if the power went out? What if it was storming and you needed to get supplies?

   Avoid: Mom, you'd call your neighbor or me if the power went out, I guess. And would you phone the grocery store for a delivery if you needed food?

   Try: Hey Dad, Rowan told me that you weren't really eating much these days. What do you typically have as a snack?

   Avoid: Hey Dad, would you snack on cheese and crackers if you got hungry?

WHEN SOMEONE ELSE IS ASSESSING YOUR PARENT'S MENTAL CAPACITY

Similar principles apply if you accompany your parent to a meeting with a medical or financial professional who's trying to assess whether they understand the information and appreciate the consequences. Even though it's hard, don't jump in to cover or prompt your parent. It isn't your meeting, and it's the professional's obligation to meet with their client in private—so don't be put off if you're asked to wait in the hall. The professional may invite you back into the room later at your parent's request.

Try: Aunt Maya, this is your meeting, so I'll just be in the hall if you need anything. Are you good for water?

Avoid: Oh, auntie, you remember that you came here to deposit that check, right? It's the one in your hand. And you wanted to give money to each of the grandkids for Christmas, too.

If you are invited into a meeting, don't take over, but do gently help orient your parent to the questions by giving them cues.

Try: Mom, I think there's something in your briefcase that you wanted to show Ms. Jones. Was it about money, maybe?

Avoid: Give me the briefcase, Mom—I'll grab that check you wanted to give Ms. Jones for cashing into small bills.

Let's talk about dementia

UNDERSTANDING DEMENTIA

When you're worried about your parent's mental state, dementia is probably your biggest concern. About one in four people over the age of eighty-five have a *diagnosis* of dementia,[2] but the real numbers are actually much higher as many people don't get properly diagnosed for reasons like shame, fear of stigma, or lack of healthcare access. And many older adults may have mild cognitive impairment (MCI), a type of "pre-dementia."

Dementia is a general term for several diseases that impact memory, thinking, and daily activities. Over time, these conditions destroy nerve cells and damage the brain, leading to serious deterioration in cognitive function far beyond the occasional "senior moments" caused by normal aging.[3] Alzheimer's disease is the type of dementia most people know, and it's also what we call dementias that are "left over" when doctors can't find a specific diagnosis.

Mostly, dementia isn't a genetic condition, but we aren't exactly sure what causes it.[4] We do know that the following factors increase its likelihood.

- High blood pressure
- Diabetes
- Being overweight
- Smoking
- Excessive alcohol consumption
- Physical inactivity
- Social isolation
- Depression[5]

Dementia's impacts usually start about ten years before a diagnosis,[6] and the "first things to go" are typically higher mental processing abilities that allow us to understand abstract problems, like dealing with finances. The effects get worse over time and are eventually fatal. However, the process can take a long time (decades, in many cases)[7]—so chances are, someone with dementia may die of another condition first.

There's currently no cure for dementia. But the first disease-modifying treatments are starting to emerge, so there's real hope for the future.

SIGNS YOUR PARENT MAY HAVE DEMENTIA

The first signs of dementia might not actually be memory loss, but rather changes to your parent's mood and personality. As you read through the common early warnings below, keep in mind that you're looking for patterns—there's no need to panic if your parent is simply having a bad week and acting cranky or crankier than usual.

Symptom	Examples
Forgetfulness	• Having issues with short-term memory of things, people, or events • Losing or misplacing items in a different way than usual • Having trouble finding words
Disorientation	• Getting lost while walking or driving • Misjudging how far away objects are • Losing a sense of time • Struggling to follow conversations
Problems with everyday activities	• Being generally confused, even in familiar places and with familiar people • Struggling to problem-solve or make decisions
Personality and mood changes	• Becoming anxious, sad, or angry about memory issues • Expressing more negative, angry emotions • Disengaging from work, activities, and relationships • Behaving inappropriately (like profane language or hypersexuality) • Focusing strongly on oneself and becoming less interested in other people[8]

IS IT REALLY DEMENTIA?

So, what do you do if you're worried your parent is "losing it"? The first step is getting your parent to a general practitioner for a full physical. You might wonder why you aren't starting with a psychiatrist or geriatrician—and you may end up there eventually. But the most frustrating thing about dementia is that it's a last-ditch diagnosis with no quick blood test to determine it. You have to rule everything else out first—and here's how to do that.

THE PHYSICAL CHECKUP

Looking for physical reasons for cognitive impairment is important because lots of other medical conditions can be mistaken for dementia. These issues can be addressed (good!), but they can cause serious problems if left unattended (not good). Here's a checklist for your parent's doctor.

- Check blood sugar levels to rule out diabetes, hypoglycemia, or hyperglycemia.

- Run a blood test and urinalysis to look for infections or chemical imbalances. Urinary tract infections are notorious for causing delirium: a temporary loss of cognitive function due to things like fevers, surgeries, or infections.[9]

- Review medications to ensure that they're not individually or collectively causing secondary mental confusion or other negative impacts:

  - Migraine medications, opioids, or certain nerve pain prescriptions can affect mental capacity[10]—anyone who's had Tylenol #3 or morphine after a dental surgery can tell you how woozy they felt, but older adults can be particularly susceptible to this side effect.

  - Don't forget non-prescription medications: Are they taking over-the-counter pills, traditional Chinese medicine, or herbal supplements?

- If your parent is diabetic, check that the type of insulin they're taking is right for them—for example, they may need to switch from short- to long-acting. Measure their blood sugar levels to ensure they're within the doctor's recommended ranges.

- Rule out post-surgical delirium: Did they just have that hip replacement you finally got them to agree to, but now they're acting really confused and odd? This is especially common for people over the age of seventy, and it often sorts itself out in a couple of days.

- Don't forget booze and recreational drugs (more on that in chapters 25 and 26).

- Look for high or low blood pressure, strokes, tumors, migraines, chronic or acute pain, and any other possible physical reasons, such as genetic or progressive diseases like Huntington's.

- Take a deep dive into your parent's nutrition and hydration—what looks like organic confusion may be malnutrition, inadequate diet, or chronic dehydration.

- Keep a lookout for sleep disorders, including sleep apnea. "My dad was always a terrible snorer" could mean that he's not getting enough sleep or taking enough oxygen into his system because he repeatedly stops breathing at night.

THE MENTAL CHECKUP

Even if the physical checkup is totally clear, you still need to rule out mental issues before landing on dementia. Consider consulting a psychiatrist to check for these if your parent's regular doctor can't find anything amiss.

The first thing to consider is depression, which is a very common condition in older adults—particularly those who have lost a spouse or friend, moved to a new location, or are socially isolated. Beyond its effects on emotions, depression significantly impacts reasoning, understanding, and appreciation.

There could also be other untreated mental health issues to consider. Although the stigma and lack of resources around mental health conditions are still profound, it was worse back when our parents were young. Many other conditions, in addition to the ones above, can cause symptoms that mimic dementia or Alzheimer's disease, including disorders of the heart, lungs, liver or kidneys, thyroid problems, sodium or vitamin D deficiency, some cancers, pain, constipation, heavy alcohol use and most of all, *depression*.[11] Also consider the following undiagnosed conditions.

- ADHD/ADD
- Autism[12]
- Bipolar disorder
- Borderline personality disorder
- Histrionic personality disorder
- PTSD/trauma[13]

YEP, IT'S PROBABLY DEMENTIA

After working through a physical and mental checkup, it's now time to look for a diagnosis of dementia. Take a deep breath: This next section isn't going to be easy, and unfortunately I don't have a ton of good jokes to help you through it.

Your parent will need a mental capacity assessment in order to be diagnosed. You'll want to be clear about what kind of assessment is happening—for instance, a "capacity assessment" may actually be a functional assessment of "activities of daily living" (ADLs), which isn't what you need.

How you get this done will depend on where you live. In some places, you can hire a mental capacity assessor as a privately paid service. But in most jurisdictions, health care providers (which may include social workers, occupational therapists, or nurses) may be able to perform a mental capacity assessment.

The gold standard is a clinical capacity assessment from a geriatric psychiatrist. You'll probably have to ask for a specific referral and be prepared to beg a bit, as these types of doctors are pretty rare. They're more common in larger urban centers with teaching hospitals, but some rural areas might have one in a regional center.

Some psychiatrists, neurologists, gerontologists, or geriatricians will also perform mental capacity assessments. Sometimes general practitioner doctors will, too—but they're unlikely to have in-depth training, as it's rare for medical students to learn this in school. If your parent's doctor says this isn't their area, trust them and get a referral. You can also reach out to local Alzheimer's associations to see if they have recommendations.

THE MENTAL CAPACITY ASSESSMENT

The two most commonly used types of mental capacity assessment are the mini–mental state examination (MMSE) and the Montreal Cognitive Assessment (MoCA).[14]

The MMSE is a quick review that provides a snapshot of potential issues to explore further. Patients are examined in many wide areas, and the specialist flags any areas that seem unusually low-functioning.

Far too often, the MMSE is the *only* test performed, which is inadequate. For example, your dad may go into an MMSE assessment while having a bad day, with his limited English and his high school education, and get a very poor score while still being mentally capable. But your mom might take the test on a good day and, combined with her excellent English and PhD in electrical engineering, she could do exceptionally well while actually being quite mentally incapable. The MMSE is only a screening test, not a determination of mental capacity. If it's the only test your parent has, you should push harder for a clinical interview or at least a deeper set of tests.

The MoCA is a standardized, sensitive screening tool that's widely used around the world and is often considered a more robust test than the MMSE. It's especially useful for detecting mild cognitive impairment (MCI), a precursor to dementia. I recommend asking for both the MMSE and the MoCA if possible.

If your parent is diagnosed with dementia, I'm sorry. This is an illness that affects not only the person who has it, but also everyone around them, and there's still a profound stigma around the disease that we need to push back against. The next chapter is full of resources that can help support both your parent and you.

9
—

How should I care for my parent who has dementia?

I can't promise that this chapter will be much fun. But it might get funny at some points—because when we're talking about dementia, we have to laugh a bit. We need all the joy and humor we can get among the realities of disconnection and worry.

Sometimes, there's the pure happiness of connecting on a "good day" by sharing an activity that brings back memories or just enjoying a nice hug. Other times, there's a sense of the hilariously and profoundly absurd—like, on occasions, you and your parent could have a conversation in which they believe it's the middle of the twentieth century while you're making plans for next week. You may occasionally find yourself inadvertently playing the role of someone else in your parent's life, like their childhood friend, parent, work colleague, or even teacher. All this can give you new insights into who they used to be when those memories were current affairs.

There's one example that always makes me smile to remember: As a university student, I volunteered in a long-term care home as a friendly visitor to a woman with dementia who had no family. The two of us had the same conversation each time, twice a week for three years. It went like this:

Me: Hi! Great to see you. My name is Laura.

Her: Really! That's amazing—that's my name, too! Do you like the smell of frying onions? Because I HATE them. They smell awful. I think maybe I've seen you before.

Me: It's lovely to see you, Laura. About those onions . . .

To keep things interesting for both of us, on Tuesdays I would agree that they smelled terrible. On Thursdays, I would protest that they smelled wonderful. All in all, I just relaxed into it and let it flow over me, acknowledging that our biweekly get-togethers felt like a cross between *Waiting for Godot* and Monty Python. The patience and hilarity I learned from my visits with "No-Onions Laura" have lasted a lifetime.

And it's *not* all loss. Some people find new creativity and hobbies, new relationships, new loves. Heck, my grandmother became a *nicer person*—we had a better, richer, warmer relationship when she had moderate dementia than when we were both younger as, frankly, she didn't have much time for female children. But I won't sugarcoat it: Dementia is hard. Warm understanding, a sense of humor, and generosity of spirit are your best tools for what's to come.

Things to do after the diagnosis

I know, the last thing you want after getting the news is another to-do list. But starting to think about these points now will help you prepare for a much less chaotic experience later—and, more importantly, improve your parent's quality of life. This to-do list is sorted roughly by priority, with the most urgent items first.

FIND YOUR LOCAL ALZHEIMER'S ORGANIZATION

Get online and search for a nearby chapter of organizations like Alzheimer's Association (in the US) or Alzheimer's Society (in Canada). These groups can provide help with navigating complex care systems and dealing with costs, and they have resources for you and your family as well as your parent.

GET REFERRALS TO HEALTH CARE PROVIDERS

The standardized tests at the end of the previous chapter might be the end of the care your parent receives unless you push for a referral to a neurologist, geriatrician, or geriatric psychiatrist. Where possible, get connected to a "hub-based clinic" that has integrated social and health care supports, testing, and monitoring all in the same place. Your parent should get an MRI of their brain soon after diagnosis, followed by regular scans to track the disease's progression.

RESEARCH TREATMENTS

Most treatments for dementia, and particularly for Alzheimer's, really only work if they're started at an early stage. Many promising options are just starting to hit the market, so you'll want to do your own research on what's available. Although there's currently no cure for dementia, these innovations can help prolong the time that your parent is healthy and cognitively intact.

PUT EVERYONE IN THERAPY

Yes, not just your parent—you, too. The future will have lots of transitions, emotions, fears, and grief for everyone to manage. People usually skip straight to focusing on physical health care and logistical concerns as a way of coping, but having help with mentally processing everything can make this tough time a bit easier.

SORT OUT FINANCIAL AND LEGAL AFFAIRS

A dementia diagnosis doesn't necessarily mean that your parent can't make or change a will, power of attorney, or other substitute decision-making document; sell property; update financial accounts or insurance policies; or get married or divorced. All this depends on what we learned in the previous chapter about your parent's ability to understand information related to a decision, appreciate the consequences, and meet any specific legal requirements in their jurisdiction.

In some cases, your parent's diagnosis will come with an official determination that they can no longer manage their own financial or health affairs. In others, you'll have to make your own judgment call. Either way, this is a good time to decide who will be the right substitute decision-maker now or in the future as your parent's capabilities change. See the sections on power of attorney (starting on page 95) for more on this.

PLAN FOR AGING IN PLACE

You might assume that a diagnosis of dementia means your parent will be quickly moving into long-term care, but actually, this is pretty unlikely. In fact, in western countries, between 60 and 75 percent of people with dementia remain at home,[1] with caregiving provided by family or friends and augmented by paid providers as things get more challenging. This number varies by country and jurisdiction and is hard to measure, but you get the idea. Lots of folks stay at home, at least until the later stages of dementia.

With this in mind, look at your parent's home and assess its suitability not just for "aging in place," but for aging in place with cognitive impairment. Chapter 1 is a good place to start.

ENCOURAGE HEALTHY LIFESTYLE CHANGES

There's nothing more annoying than being told to "eat right and exercise," but in this case, it really does help. Brain health is body health, so good nutrition, regular cardio exercise, and opportunities to learn new things are all important here. You can't necessarily make your parent do these things, but you can reverse the script from your childhood by occasionally nagging them to eat healthy foods and get outdoors. At the same time, you should encourage your parent to work with their doctor to avoid issues like medication interactions or unstable blood sugar that can make the health problems they're already dealing with worse—see chapter 21 for more.

PROMOTE SOCIAL ENGAGEMENT

Active engagement with others makes a world of difference for anyone, but especially for people with dementia, touch, emotional connection, and social inclusion are key. You can help your parent create a regular routine of visits with family and friends, both in person and virtually. Also, encourage them to keep seeking out new experiences, like a walking group or faith-based meetings. Try not to worry about awkward social stumbling blocks like whether your parent can remember someone's name—the people who are there for them will understand.

USE SUPPORTIVE TECHNOLOGY

Likewise, everyone can benefit from staying organized with notes and reminders, but they're all-important for helping people with cognitive impairment maintain everyday health and independence. I'm talking about smartphone calendar alerts, old-fashioned written lists, and structured daily routines (like pills being set out by your parent's toothbrush in the morning so they remember to take their meds while getting ready). You'll want to introduce your parent to these aids early on to create automatic patterns that will help when their cognition starts to decline later.

Understanding your parent's behavior

As your parent's health changes, their behavior might also shift in ways that can feel confusing and scary. People with dementia are often hyper-stimulated and easily startled, which can sometimes cause them to lash out. But it's still totally possible for you and your parent to have positive interactions, and this advice can help.

PHYSICAL CONTACT

To avoid surprising them, always approach a person with dementia from the front, but not directly. Remember when you learned to drive and were told to keep your hands at ten and two on the wheel? Walk up to your parent from either of those directions. Use a warm tone, and don't touch them unannounced. Instead, gently and slowly lay your hand on their upper arm. Invite and guide rather than direct or push.

SENSORY EXPERIENCES

People with dementia often feel better when they have something to do with their hands. Consider getting your parent squishy, soft, or spiky stress balls, or "twiddle muffs": knitted fabric tubes that have things to fiddle with sewn inside. For another sensory experience, people with dementia find weighted blankets soothing—but for others, they may be claustrophobic, so pay attention to your parent's reactions.

Overly bright lights are often irritating . . . well, for just about everyone, but particularly for people with dementia. Consider putting warm gels over their home's lights or changing the bulbs entirely. Don't make it dim, just less fluorescent and overwhelming.

WANDERING/EXPLORING

Walking, or "wandering," is a favorite activity for many people with dementia, and it can be quite wonderful for them to have a safe meandering path indoors or outside. If you can, design easy-to-follow outdoor loops or guided walkways through a garden. Occasional benches and handrails are useful for rest and safety.

Color-coding can provide visual cues that help your parent get around their living space. Consider using navigational markings (like those in hospitals or airports) on inside or outside floors to help with directions. Inside the house, color-coded low-pile carpet or inlaid tile can help people with dementia tell different parts of a residence apart.

ENGAGING TASKS

Doing nothing is the worst, so creating opportunities for your parent to participate in familiar tasks is often helpful. Activities like gardening, "office work," or even organizing supplies can be calming and purposeful. Consider your parent's routine in their younger life: If they went to the office every day, you could re-create that experience in their home by setting up a room with office furniture, paper, and whatever tools of the trade that are safe and useful for them.

TIME OF DAY

Many people with dementia have times of day when they feel better or worse. "Sundowning" is common: feeling good in the morning but becoming more agitated (including wandering or getting upset) in the afternoon or evening. Try to plan activities according to the rhythms of your parent's day and see if it helps them to rest in the early afternoon before sundowning starts.

Dos and don'ts

Do: Encourage your parent to chat about whatever comes to their mind, even if they get names, places, or past events mixed up.

Don't: Argue, correct them, or insist that they're wrong—it's unnecessarily frustrating for everyone and gets you nowhere.

Do: Reminisce about your parent's childhood or work life, particularly moments from the past that spark them to engage in activities now.

Don't: Ask about the specifics of their day today, since their poor short-term memory can cause frustration.

Do: Ask how your parent is feeling and get them to show you places or activities they enjoy. Follow their lead.

Don't: Quiz them on specific details of appointments or activities.

Do: Speak clearly with a warm, friendly tone.

Don't: Mumble while looking angry or upset.

Do: Focus on one idea or question at a time.

Don't: Jam together several ideas in one sentence.

Do: Take your parent out for exercise, to visit nature, and engage in activities like gardening, cooking, or sharing meals.

Don't: Bring them into busy, loud, and confusing areas or take trips with multiple stops.

Do: Look for ways for your parent to find joy and reduce agitation. Appreciate the time you have together.

Don't: Be weepy and talk about how much they have "lost."

Common problems and solutions

SHAME AND STIGMA

Although there's often a depressing amount of shame or stigma attached to it, dementia is like any other health condition—there's nothing for your parent, or you, to be ashamed of at all.

If you don't like your parent being referred to as a "person living with dementia," or if the "D word" is too upsetting for your family, consider being factual about symptoms when your parent is interacting with new people. It could sound something like this:

"My dad is active and engaged and would love to be included. He has a bit of a hard time with short-term memory and can sometimes get confused during conversations. It's best if he's talking one-on-one in a gentle, flowing way rather than having a 'what did you do today' kind of talk. He can remember things from his early years, and he's a great storyteller, too."

BEHAVIORAL RESPONSES

No one likes to hear that their kid hit someone at preschool, and no one likes to get a call from a long-term care facility telling you that your parent smacked another resident. You might feel upset, helpless, embarrassed, or concerned that they're going to be removed from their care home.

But there's good news: Behavioral responses can often be managed with trained staff, calming techniques, and redirecting activities. In the rare cases where they can't be handled with those tools, you might need to have conversations about the possibility of restraints, antipsychotic medication, or locked wards. Try to avoid these measures at all costs, as they're generally unhelpful and may cause your parent more distress. Your first step should be working with your parent's care team to follow the problem-solving approach below, which is used in some form by Alzheimer's organizations across the world.

- **Identify the problem:** Name and describe your parent's unwanted behavior.

- **Analyze the problem:** Ask yourself questions about this behavior. What factors (like other people, their environment, or medical issues) might be contributing to their reaction? What is your parent trying to communicate?

- **List possible strategies:** Think of all the ways to possibly solve the problem, keeping in mind the kind of support your parent currently has and what additional resources you could add.

- **Choose a strategy:** Weigh the pros and cons of each strategy before selecting one.
- **Take action:** Put the chosen strategy into effect.
- **Assess the results:** Did the strategy work? If not, why not?

Of course, this approach might not work on your first try. Trial and error plus specialist consultations with health care workers or other dementia experts can really help.

If restraints do have to be involved, use the least restrictive option first. For instance, instead of giving your parent tranquilizers to prevent wandering, consider putting a code-operated lock on your parent's door that only staff members can open.

Making the most of your time with your parent

Dementia is a long road to travel down, so find still points throughout the journey by paying attention to moments of calm—from a silly conversation to a tender hug. Getting inspiration for activities from these following themes can help bring more moments of joy to your interactions with your parent, too.

FOOD

Food (and the smell of food!) is so important to identity and culture. Cooking or baking together doesn't just give you an opportunity to connect, it also prompts your parent's brain and stomach to eat regularly.

You may need to help them use the stovetop or oven and take over steps that involve using sharp objects or measuring ingredients. Also, if you need assistance to ensure your parent can eat the food you prepare, check with a dietitian or nutritionist. Texture and swallowing are common challenges, but often there are ways to puree foods that still keep the flavors alive.

NATURE

Walking together, getting exercise, and exploring the green spaces in the local community are enormously good for everyone. You could wade in a pond, take a horse-drawn carriage through the park, or ride bicycles or tricycles. If restaurants are too loud and confusing for your parent, you can take the opportunity to have a picnic together outdoors.

Even if your parent never had a green thumb before, gardening can also be a wonderfully therapeutic way of spending time. Small, easy activities like planting, deadheading flowers, growing herbs or vegetables, and digging in the earth are both hugely satisfying and quite literally grounding. Grandkids and other younger relatives will have fun with this one, too!

MEDIA

When looking for TV shows and movies to watch or books to read together, choose shorter options. Visual media that's less stimulating is better—nature documentaries or travel shows are great choices.

Music and dance are also excellent ways to connect. The part of our brains that engages in these activities is not as affected by dementia,[2] so even mostly nonverbal people can often "come back to life" and start singing old songs from their childhood or bust out some dance moves from their youth. Try making a playlist with favorites from your parent's early years.

CRAFTS

Working on an artistic project together can be lovely, or you can organize a craft group and create things separately. Textile art like knitting or embroidery is especially engaging for people with dementia because of the soothing sensory stimulation. You can also use old photographs and mementos to create scrapbooks about your parent's life.

Dementia is hard—I won't say anything different. Trying to find pleasure in your time with your parent takes both patience and a willingness to live in the time in which your parent thinks they're existing. "Now" is a fixed concept I strongly suggest you let go of, because dementia teaches us all to be existentialists in our own way and connect to our essential selves. Love has no time zone or year, you aren't alone, and you're doing great.

10

What are powers of
attorney (POA)?

What can I say about powers of attorney? I can say that they're important, but only between 11 and 40 percent of adults in western countries have them.[1] I can say that they make things much easier—unless your parent picks someone who's a nightmare for the job and makes everything worse. (I know you're thinking of that one particular family member . . . and now you're getting annoyed imagining how bad they would be.) I can also say that they're essential documents for protecting people like your parent—unless they're used for abuse. It's complicated.

No matter where you live, powers of attorney do essentially the same thing: They're legal documents made by a mentally capable adult that pick someone to make decisions if that adult can't (or, in some rare cases, if they just prefer not to).

In some jurisdictions, there are two documents: one covering health and personal care decisions, including housing, and another covering property and financial decisions. More rarely, there may be just one document with two parts.

Typically, when someone creates a POA document, they choose another person to speak for them—to essentially step into their shoes. This person is called the attorney. (This can be confusing, since that is also what lawyers are known as. I straighten that out in the "Definitions to Know" box.) In certain jurisdictions, one can create a document that directly instructs a third-party doctor, lawyer, or financial advisor—this is sometimes called an "advance directive" or "living will."

POAs are for when someone is alive, while wills are for when they're dead. When the person granting the POA dies, that authority dies, too.

Why do we use them?

We most often think of using POA when an aging parent loses mental capacity and isn't able to make their own legal decisions about finances, health care, or housing.

Without POA, no one is going to pay the bills if you're in a coma or have advanced dementia. Most people assume that they can waltz into the bank and say, "Hey, I'm Florence's daughter, and I'm here to take over her finances." No—absolutely not.

POAs can be used for scenarios that aren't quite so medically dire, too. For instance, your mom and dad could go on a trip to Europe and tell you that if you need to pay the contractor for their home renovation, you can simply use the POA for property and financial issues and pay out of your parents' bank account. I myself used this strategy so my husband could stand in an endless line to renew my parking pass at city hall because I didn't want to do it and he occasionally proves his love for me through acts of civic administration. (To be fair, it was during COVID-19 in the middle of an icy winter, and he had to renew his own, too. Thanks to my POA for property, I stayed at home snuggled up with my dog.)

It's likely that you or a sibling will end up being a substitute decision-maker for your parent, but most of us aren't prepared for this and frankly haven't got a clue about what the job really entails. It can be a real pain in the butt to be an attorney, since it takes time, effort, and sometimes very specific accounting requirements.

To help sort all this out, we're going to talk about what POAs are and aren't, plus why you probably should have them. (Yes, you too, not just your parents. Oh, and your adult children as well, if you have them.)

Grantor: The person who creates a POA document and "grants" someone the authority to make decisions on their behalf.

Attorney: The person appointed by the grantor to be a substitute decision-maker. In this context, the word "attorney" has nothing to do with being a lawyer.

POA for personal care/health care (aka representation agreement, personal directive, or health care directive): Covers substitute decisions related to health care, living situation (like housing), home care, lifestyle decisions, and food requirements.

POA for property: Covers substitute decisions related to real estate, finances, business matters, bank accounts, investments, and other property, including valuable items like cars and jewelry.

Advance directive/living will: Avoids appointing a substitute decision-maker by giving instructions directly to a health care provider or legal or financial professional.

Will: Outlines what to do with someone's property after their death but has no power when they are alive. The person appointed to distribute the deceased person's *estate* is the *executor*.

Who gets to make decisions and when?

A mentally capable adult always gets to make their own property and personal care decisions—even if friends or family don't agree with those choices. Generally, only a mentally capable adult can decide to make a POA or will, and they can also choose to change or cancel those documents at any time.

An attorney can make only the type of decisions specified in the POA, and only while the grantor is alive. On the other hand, as the executor of your parent's will, you have no substitute decision-making authority at all—your authority begins only when your parent dies.

Frequently asked questions

Q: I'm the attorney for my mom. She's still mentally capable, but she wants me to help her with finances. Can I do that?

A: Yes. As long as the document says that it's a "continuing," "enduring," or "durable" POA for property, your authority starts as soon as it's signed and executed.

Q: My dad wants to appoint both my brother and me to be his attorneys. Do we have to agree on everything, or can just one of us make a decision?

A: Your dad can appoint both of you as his attorneys. He'll have to make clear in his POA document how you and your brother must make decisions. If your dad says that you're "joint" attorneys, you need to be in unanimous agreement, but if you're "joint and several" attorneys (or similar phrasing), only one of you is needed to make a decision. I call it "first to the bank, first to the bedside."

Q: My mom has seven kids. Can she appoint all of us to be her attorneys?

A: Legally, yes—but this is a recipe for disaster. Help your mom narrow down who is best suited to each job. Is your brother Brad a financial disaster? Don't pick him to be the POA for property and finance. Is your sister Anna in medical school? Maybe choose her to be the POA for health and personal care issues.

Q: If I live far away, can I become an attorney and perform my duties remotely?

A: Some jurisdictions allow attorneys to live anywhere, while others require an attorney to reside in the same state or country as the grantor, so check the rules in your parent's location.

Q: This is a lot of work. Can I be paid for my time?

A: This also depends on your jurisdiction. Often, the government will define a set percentage or amount that can be paid to "voluntary" attorneys.

Q: I feel totally unprepared to be an attorney. Do I have to do it?

A: The answer is almost always no. You can't be forced to do it, and you can change your mind even if you agreed to act as an attorney earlier.

Q: Can I hire someone to help, or even to do the whole job for me?

A: It depends. You can usually hire someone like a lawyer or accountant to help you get the books in order. In most western countries, financial or banking institutions can be appointed in a POA for property and finance. These institutions will charge a percentage determined by government requirements. In some jurisdictions, you can hire someone to be your substitute decision-maker—this is a professional fiduciary or financial guardian, who essentially takes guardianship over your parent and their money. In the United States, your parent can also hire a professional guardian to make substitute health and personal care choices.

Great—now you know the POA basics. In the next chapter, we'll use this information to make sure your parent has up-to-date POA documents squared away.

11

What if my parent doesn't have POA set up, and when is it too late to do this?

If a parent doesn't set up POA before the car accident that puts them in a coma, or before the Alzheimer's that impairs their mental capacity, things can get tricky. Hopefully this hasn't happened yet, so I'm going to scare you with how complicated the situation could become, then help you avoid it. By the end of this section, you'll hopefully have convinced your parent to create their POA.

But let's go back to the worst-case scenario for a moment: Who becomes the decision-maker for someone without POA? A lot of this depends on your particular jurisdiction, so check your local laws. Legislation about health care consent or adult guardianship will specify a default decision-maker, but usually, there isn't a list of backup decision-makers for property or finances.

If there's no default decision-maker and your parent is no longer mentally capable, then you need to be appointed as a legal substitute. Depending on the system in your area, this may mean appearing before an administrative board or tribunal, or even in court. Unfortunately, this can be time-consuming, expensive, and exhausting, and it can cause complications if there's more than one person who wants to make the decisions.

Signs it's time to have the conversation

This is easy: If you're over the age of majority in your jurisdiction, you should have powers of attorney. (And for that matter, make a will, too. Grown-ups have wills.) It's not just older people who get sick, have psychotic episodes, or become cognitively impaired by dementia, delirium, or injury. If you know your parent doesn't have POA set up (or updated to fit their current situation), the right time is right now.

Preparing for the conversation

Before starting the main talk, work with your parent to check whether they have any previous POA documents. If you find one, look at the date (in case your family situation has changed a lot in the ten years since it was drawn up) and see if it covers financial and property issues, health and personal care issues, or both. If it's a POA for property and financial issues, check whether it's active right away and continues into incapacity, or if it "springs" into effect after a mental capacity assessment. Also look for an attached "wishes" document or a letter detailing specific things your parent wants or doesn't want done. As a bonus, you can also figure out whether your parent has an up-to-date will.

If you don't turn up any existing documents, dig around in your memory to see if you can recall ever talking about estate planning with your parent as POA often get discussed during these talks. And if you can't get the information directly from your parent, see what other family members know.

These three points are key for preparing.

Assess the context—why is the discussion happening now? Is there a health crisis or key life event on the horizon, such as a surgery, a move to long-term care, or the death of a spouse?

Determine the urgency. If your parent already has POA but wants to tweak some of the wording, that's much less time-sensitive than if they've just been diagnosed with dementia but have no POA.

Figure out the jurisdiction, checking the laws where your parent lives. If they have previous POA from another state, province, or country, those POA probably won't work as well in their current residence. Getting extra-jurisdictional recognition of a foreign POA can be done, but it's complex, time-consuming, and usually expensive.

Before you get into the discussion, you should also decide whether you want to be your parent's attorney, or if it should be someone else. It can be a tough job, so think hard about the pros and cons.

Reasons to be an attorney	Reasons not to be an attorney
• You can help a family member in a vulnerable position. • You can help yourself by regularly practicing your great organizational skills (okay, this may be a bit of a stretch). • You can be compensated for your time (but probably not what you think your time is actually worth!). • You can ensure the grantor and their dependents have their future interests looked after. • You want to swap jobs. (Maybe your family member will agree to be your attorney, too!)	• If you don't do the job correctly, you could get in trouble with the law and end up liable for any financial damages you cause. • You have to spend a lot of time keeping a careful record of any money you spend or personal care decisions you make on the grantor's behalf. • You may face conflicts with other people who have an interest in the grantor's property, like family members, friends, businesspeople, or even people to whom they owe money. • It's usually a hard job.

Whether or not you're going to take on the job, you should make a list of potential backup attorneys. There should always be at least one included in a POA document in case the primary attorney can no longer do the job (or is simply unavailable because they're hiking in the Andes). I'm overly cautious, so I have two backups, one of whom I don't travel with.

Strategies for having the conversation

When you've done all your homework, use the context and urgency you just determined as jumping-off points for your talk.

THE "PRESSING ISSUE" APPROACH

Try talking about your parent's current life change or imminent event on the horizon as a reason to look through their POA and think through any changes or new documents that might be needed. For instance, if your parent is moving into a seniors' home or long-term care, you can inform them that those homes strongly suggest (and come darn near requiring, even though they're not usually *allowed* to) POA.

If someone was previously appointed as an attorney but has passed away or becomes mentally incapable, discuss how this changes things. Spouses often pick each other as the primary attorney, so if your mom had appointed your dad as her attorney for property and finance, but now he has significant medical issues that no longer make him a good choice, you can gently use that angle.

THE "ESTATE PLANNING" APPROACH

When your parent is working on financial planning or taxes, a financial or legal professional will likely ask about POA. If you want to make sure that your dad's tax person brings this up, consider discussing it with the tax adviser first where you share your concerns about whether your dad's POA is up-to-date. Your parent may listen to their financial or legal professional long before they pay attention to you, even if *you* are a financial or legal professional. (Yes, this is close to home for me. How did you guess?)

THE "IMPENDING DISASTER" APPROACH

This is for the issues that you can see going horribly wrong from a mile away. For instance, if you know your mom has previously appointed (or is likely to appoint) your unsuccessful freeloading brother who moved into her basement while continuing his gambling habit, then it's time to take action. Or if your sister has hated your father for years and continues to blame him for a harsh childhood, then it's time to take a hard look at whether or not she should be involved in his financial or health decisions. (It's not strictly legal to be "out to get" the person you're supposed to be protecting, but it can open the possibility of "payback.")

Try to map out some trainwrecks on which you and your parent both agree. Focus on solving problems rather than assigning blame. For example, if your cousin is dealing with drug or alcohol abuse, you can ask, "How can we make sure POA decisions won't be affected by those issues?" or say, "Let's figure out how to keep the burden of being an attorney off him, since he's going through a lot right now." If you know your stepfather wants to get his hands on your mother's jewelry even though it's promised to your daughter, you could try, "Let's take pictures and make sure that everyone knows what you want to go to each person. We can attach that list to your will to make things simple."

THE "I'LL SHOW YOU MINE IF YOU SHOW ME YOURS" APPROACH

This approach requires you to start thinking about your own POA needs. Maybe you can bring your planning documents with you to ask your aunt for advice. If you're lucky, this can lead to getting your documents sorted out at the same time.

Once your parent has their POA plans settled, congratulate yourself on making your future a lot easier by averting all kinds of tricky situations. Of course, not even the most airtight legal document can prevent family members from arguing . . . so, head to the next chapter to learn about dealing with common POA-related conflicts.

12

What if my family argues about POA?

I'm always baffled as to why most folks want the job of being an attorney. It mostly sucks—it takes up a lot of time, you have to be oh so careful about the decisions you make, you need to keep detailed records, and thank-yous are nearly nonexistent. In my case, I don't mind making health care decisions, but I don't have a lot of time to drive around attending my parent's medical appointments. Most of all, I loathe detailed bookkeeping and live in fear of having to account for every single expense. "Bandages: $2.39. Must pay with this specific account and enter the transaction, with accompanying receipt, into the POA logbook." And in the fine print: If you do it wrong, you can get in trouble with the civil courts or even the police. No thanks!

Usually people's reasons are something like "Everyone else would be worse, so I guess I'll do it," or "I'm a good grown-up adult, and I *should* do these things for my parent. Even if they don't want me to and frankly might resent it."

And yet, about half the time, there's still a family member who thinks they should've been the attorney and can't accept that they weren't chosen—or just wants to have a say in all the attorney's decisions without actually taking on the responsibility. Or sometimes, the attorney who does end up getting chosen doesn't even have the mental or emotional fortitude to take care of their own affairs, let alone their parent's personal and financial decisions.

Arguments about POA tend to center on a few general themes like these, and below I've outlined how to deal with each one. I'm basing my advice on the assumption that you're the one saddled with the attorney job, but you can easily modify these scripts for use as a helpful/nosy bystander, too. Hopefully, we'll get through this with as much poise, gravitas, and understanding as possible—which will keep you from bashing your head against a wall in sheer frustration.

"It should have been me."

Some folks take real offense when they're not chosen to be the substitute decision-maker for their parent. There's a sense that if you aren't chosen, your parent doesn't trust or love you, or they don't think you're reliable enough to handle their money. The "it should have been me" narrative is often a cover-up for feeling hurt, pushed aside, or undermined. It can really rattle how an adult child views their relationship with their parent, and it may also bring back childhood fears or frustration about birth order or gender roles.

WHAT TO DO

If you're the person who *was* chosen (or even just a family member or friend of the person who was passed over), listen to them. Are they scared? Are they worried about the state of the relationship? Are they offended that they didn't get picked? Or are they legitimately concerned that their parent picked a really bad person with terrible judgment to be their attorney? Validate and help them name their feelings.

If you feel that *you* shouldn't have been chosen and you don't want the job, you can decline the position at any time. Typically, it will then go to the backup person already listed on the POA.

If you think your upset family member is wrong, you can talk a little about why your parent might have chosen you.

"I'm a chartered accountant, so it's really easy for me to do all the tedious money stuff."

"Mom probably picked me since I live so close by, so it's simple for me to run over for a quick errand or appointment."

You can also simply ignore their objections—it all depends on the relationships involved.

WHAT NOT TO DO

- Depending on your relationship, if none of the previous suggestions work, you may have to eventually just ignore their protests . . . but this should be your last resort.

- Say, "Why would you even want to be the attorney, anyway? It's a terrible job."

- Mock them, even as a joke. ("See, your dad always liked your brother more than you!")

"I don't want to make decisions, but I don't want anyone else to, either."

This type of reaction might feel petty, snarky, and passive-aggressive. (And it could *be* all of those things, too!) However, it could be a real, profound denial of your aging parent's actual situation. What may look like cranky or unreasonable behavior could be a way to avoid pain by pretending your parent isn't succumbing to disease or forgetfulness.

WHAT TO DO

If your relative is the snippy, snarky type, you've probably dealt with this your entire life and may have some defense strategies you can dust off. But if you can, try to meet them on an emotional level. Perhaps you could share how you're feeling about the situation and invite them to do the same. Put aside the POA topic and say that you appreciate them and really see how much they care. Be warm and calm and maintain boundaries. Deep breaths and all that.

If they're someone who likes concrete plans, consider working with them to create a roadmap document for guiding substitute decision-making. A few written "what if" scenarios, plus some resources from your local jurisdiction about the responsibilities of an attorney, can be useful. The substitute decision-maker is responsible for getting input from others anyway, so you'll just be doing your job.

WHAT NOT TO DO

- Meet snark with snark. (They're not a seven-year-old sticking their wet finger in your ear anymore. Okay, maybe *they* still act like it, but *you* aren't going to. You are above slap-fights and hair-pulling even if you might mentally indulge in the fantasy.)

- Ignore their denial, grief, or fear just because those issues are coming out in an irritating way.

"We have to 'jointly' agree on decisions— but we don't agree at all (and might fight to the death)!"

About half of POA documents have a "joint" decision-making provision. In many jurisdictions, this is the default that will go into effect unless your parent changes it to "joint and several."

If you and your family members are "joint" substitute decision-makers, you will all need to reach a consensus on each decision. If you can't do this, it can get nasty and expensive—you'll likely need to go to court and apply for a court-ordered guardianship that trumps the POA. If that happens, you're looking at wasting tens of thousands of dollars and never getting invited back home for the holidays.

WHAT TO DO

This is pretty obvious, but in case you've blown right past it, ask the dissenter about their reasoning in a warm, kind, respectful fashion.

You can also find out if anyone who isn't listed on the POA has insight into your parent's values, wishes, and beliefs. Ask their best friends or siblings, since more ideas sometimes shake a deadlock loose. Double-check to see if there's an "in case of deadlock, break glass" clause in the POA—it might go something like, "If my kids Anne and Frances can't agree jointly, my best friend Shane gets to make the decision."

If things still aren't going well, you can ask each other if one of you should step away from making this particular decision, "abstaining" in one instance while keeping your attorney powers overall. One of you could also resign the attorney position entirely, but you'll need to consult a legal professional to understand how that would affect the POA itself—does the other person immediately get ongoing authority, or does the document collapse and the decision go to court? Separately, your jurisdiction may allow everyone to agree to turn over decision-making to a professional guardian, fiduciary, or trust company.

Reinforce your understanding of your obligations as well as what happens if attorneys can't agree by consulting a lawyer, a social worker, or free legal educational resources. You could even hire a mediator to help you have a constructive discussion and come up with a plan of action. When bringing something like this up, it can help to highlight how useful their extra knowledge will be to everyone.

"There's a lot at stake here, and we all want to do the right thing for Dad. So, I think we need a bit more advice to help us think this through."

Remember that you're always required to "stand in the shoes" of the grantor, and you're not supposed to bring your own values into the decision.

For instance, your mom might have specified that she wanted all possible medical care, including blood transfusions. Now she's been put under anesthetic for a routine procedure, and it's gone south: She needs to go on a ventilator for a few days and get that transfusion.

You say, "Mom always said she didn't want to be on a ventilator, but she meant long-term, not for a day or two. Also, she asked for every possible medical measure to be taken." Your sister, who joined the Jehovah's Witnesses, might be OK with the ventilator for a short duration, but she's absolutely opposed to the blood transfusion, since it's against her faith. Remember—it's not *her* preferences that should be guiding the decision.

WHAT NOT TO DO

- Threaten to go to court, except as a *very* last resort.

- Take the argument to social media (or the actual media) unless there's an overwhelming reason to do so. You can never take this back.

- Make derogatory remarks. ("You must not know Grandpa very well if you think that's what he'd want!")

- Take over and go behind the other attorneys' backs to enforce your preferences. Legally, you aren't ever allowed to do this.

"Whose version of the POA is the real POA?"

There are a couple of scenarios where more than one POA document covering the same type of decisions might be floating around. Whether this is for shady reasons, like in the first scenario below, or good ones, as in the second scenario, things can get confusing:

SCENARIO 1

You have one set of POA documents that were done by a lawyer ten years ago, appointing you as your mom's attorney. You do your duty and work hard to make the right decisions according to her preferences and in her best interests. Then, one day, your ne'er-do-well nephew shows up and hands you a copy of new POA documents appointing him as your mom's attorney. You don't know if the new documents are even legal, and you don't know if your mom, who has fluctuating mental capacity, would even be able to understand and appreciate what it means to make a new POA, anyway.

What to do

Typically (but not always), the creation of new POA documents automatically revokes any old ones. Hold on to copies of both your original documents and your nephew's, then make an appointment with a lawyer to get them all checked out. If you have any kind of assertion from a medical or legal professional that your mom isn't mentally competent to appoint an attorney, you'll want to bring this up.

What not to do

- Ignore the situation and assume that because your nephew's POA forms look questionable, no one will actually abide by them.

- There's not a lot you *shouldn't* do, here—it's an emergency situation for sure!

SCENARIO 2

Your uncle is worried that your brother has been inappropriate in his use of the POA for financial and property issues. He thinks that money might be going missing, so he wants to change the POA and appoint you instead.

What to do

Your first goal here is ensuring that your uncle's property is safe from your brother's sketchy dealings, but you'll also want to avoid making it look like you're trying to inappropriately influence your uncle yourself. You should send him to a lawyer for independent advice—ideally, someone else will drive him to the appointment, but if you have to be the one who comes along, you should at least wait outside the room where it's all going down. While the lawyer is drawing up new documents, they will also determine your uncle's mental capacity and screen for undue influence or abuse.

If you live in a jurisdiction where a legal professional is not needed to assign POA, your uncle could create his own documents using a standardized legal form. This can be useful if cost, timing, or distance prevent hiring a lawyer, but on the other hand, having a lawyer involved makes the whole thing so much safer and easier to uphold under scrutiny from judges, police, or even just other family members. Keep in mind that many lawyers do POA documents and wills as "loss leaders," offering a package deal at a very reasonable price (although if your situation is particularly complicated, then I'd highly recommend you hire a specialist focusing on wills, trusts, and estates).

What not to do

- Argue with your uncle and try to convince him that you'll make sure your brother handles his funds correctly. As long as your uncle is mentally capable, the choice of attorney is his.

- Help your uncle draw up his new DIY POA documents himself—remember, we want you to be as impartial as possible here.

Who to tell about new powers of attorney

In any situation where new POA documents are in place, you should send letters confirming that the old ones are revoked and provide copies of the new ones. Where should these letters go? Banks, investment managers, pension funds, tax filing offices, insurance offices, lawyers, health care providers, retirement home administrators, utility companies, or charities your parent donates to all might require notification. I recommend asking that the old POA documents be returned to you—or, if you sent electronic files, asking the third party to confirm in writing that they've deleted those files and started using the updated documents.

"You're doing a bad job and should stop being the attorney."

Regularly, one family member or close friend will look at the decisions (or lack of decisions) being made by the attorney and come to the conclusion that the attorney is doing it wrong. There may be valid concerns that elder financial abuse is occurring: assets are going awry, bills aren't being paid, or zero record-keeping is being done. There could be legitimate worry that your parent with dementia is losing weight, hasn't been seeing a doctor regularly, and is left in their home unattended.

Well, sometimes this is true, and sometimes not so much—these concerns could stem from false impressions brought on by worry, a lack of insight into the situation, or a lack of trust in the decision-maker. When concerns like these come up, it's always important to find out what's going on for sure, since your parent could be in physical or financial danger.

I'm writing this section as though you're a concerned outside family member, not the no-good attorney. If you are acting as the attorney, you'll want to keep a careful record of all the decisions you've made with accompanying receipts (see my gripe about accounting for the cost of bandages at the start of this chapter) that you can share with loved ones who are worried about your parent's care—or with medical or legal authorities if it becomes necessary.

Even if you do decide an attorney isn't taking proper care of your parent's affairs, you'll need to prepare yourself for a scenario where the concerns *are* warranted, *and yet* they don't reach a high enough standard for legally challenging the attorney's authority. You might think the decisions are poor or even stupid, but a lawyer might disagree, leaving you to use diplomacy instead.

WHAT TO DO

How aggressively you attack this problem is really going to depend on your particular circumstances and how hard you (or your other relatives) are willing or able to push the issue.

What do I mean? Well, for instance, let's go back to the example of an attorney for property and financial decisions mismanaging your parent's funds. We'll say your sister the attorney is stealing gambling money from your mom's accounts.

You could dramatically confront her with the evidence—or, if you think that approach won't work and would likely make things worse, you could play your cards close to your chest and contact the police or adult protective services (or a public guardian and trustee, or a regional health authority). To find out who to call in your jurisdiction, you can search online for your national or local elder abuse prevention network—typing "who do I report elder abuse to in [location]" will get the results you need. Unfortunately, whether or not the response will be timely, affordable, or practical is entirely another story.

Another method is showing up at your mom's for a visit, since just being there and asking questions could make your sister uncomfortable enough that she slows down or stops her unsavory conduct. This typically only works if a purposeful abuser thinks they're likely to be caught and experience consequences. Otherwise, she'll likely pull a trick from the elder abuse how-to handbook and accuse *you* of being the abuser with the tried-and-true "no defense like a good offense" tactic.

Ultimately, if your parent is mentally incapable, you may have to apply to the courts to get the existing POA overturned and have yourself appointed as the new substitute decision-maker. Like I said before, this can be a massive, expensive headache, but in cases like the one I've outlined here, you may be allowed to use some of your parent's funds to correct the situation.

WHAT NOT TO DO

- Accuse someone of being a bad attorney based only on worry or hearsay. Arguments like these can really damage families, so you should investigate the situation yourself before bringing up concerns or introducing outside authorities.

- Try to take over decisions from the attorney without going through proper legal channels to get new POA documents drawn up.

- If you're the one accused of being a bad attorney, brush off others' concerns. If they're acting in good faith, sitting them down and walking them through your plan for your parent's care can help calm their fears.

Even while you're battling through confusing legal requirements and maddening family drama, try to keep the most important thing at the front of everyone's minds: your parent's welfare. If you're focusing on that and sticking to your jurisdiction's guidelines as best you can, don't be too hard on yourself, either— because if anyone knew how to get your entire family to agree on something 100 percent, with no hurt feelings, I probably wouldn't need to write this book!

13

Is my parent getting scammed,
and what can I do about it?

I don't know about you, but I have won lotteries that I didn't enter in at least twenty-seven different countries. I've apparently inherited money from relatives I didn't know about, and I can get that inheritance if I just send some modest legal fees and proof of identity by clicking this handy link. My grandchildren (which I do not have) have repeatedly called in muffled, pleading tones asking me to help them get out of jail by wiring them money. (I've also been called by people asking for help getting out of jail in real life. Then again, I'm a lawyer—but I'm hardly old enough to have grandchildren, so get lost, fraudsters!)

You get the idea: Scam attempts happen just about every day to nearly everyone you've ever met. In the United States alone, consumers reported losing almost $8.8 billion in 2022, up 30 percent from 2021's losses.[1] But these schemes are often especially targeted toward seniors, for a few main reasons.

- Seniors often have more accrued wealth than younger people.
- Many older people have a habit of being polite to random phone callers or people who show up to ring their doorbell.
- Most seniors are less comfortable with digital communication like text messages, emails, or apps with chat features.
- Older people can be more susceptible to emotional ploys due to loneliness, lack of social support, or cognitive impairment that compromises critical thinking.

Since you're the (relatively) tech-savvy younger person, it's partly your responsibility to help your parent avoid falling victim to scammers—and pitch in to deal with the fallout if the worst does end up happening.

Signs it's time to have the conversation

Your parent has certainly already been targeted, and they may have already fallen for a scam, knowingly or unknowingly. Not only is it time for the conversation, it is also a dialogue that needs to be ongoing, since the sophistication and range of tricks are ever-growing.

Your parent might be skeptical if you tell them that they're likely already receiving all kinds of online scam attempts, since most of them get screened out by spam filters. Have you ever had a good look at their email's junk folder? You could start by doing this with your parent to show them what these types of messages look like. Some scams also get identified by warnings on your mobile phone when a sketchy number is calling. (Although telecom companies have done remarkably little in the past to identify or address scammers, many governments are now starting to put increased pressure on those businesses to protect consumers including more vulnerable groups like seniors, which is great news.)

Security pro tip

You know those "games" on social media where you're asked to fill in the name of your first pet, your favorite elementary school teacher, your lucky numbers, the street where you used to live as a child, the number of kids you have, or the year you were born? Make sure your parent knows that most of these "games" originate from scammers scraping together information to crack your login details or figure out the answers to your security questions.

Preparing for the conversation

You're probably already familiar with some scams that have crossed your path, but here's a mini prep course on some of the most common ones your parent might encounter.[2]

RED FLAGS

Unsolicited communication: Your parent might get an unexpected phone call, email, text message, or even an old-fashioned letter asking them to sign up for something or call someone about urgently needed "missing information." They should know to always contact the organization themselves rather than following along with what the unsolicited message asks—for example, if it's a text "from the bank," they should call the phone number on their bank card instead of responding.

Requests for personal or financial information: Your parent should be especially wary of requests for their date of birth, address, ID number, banking details, credit card information, or passwords. Legitimate companies will never ask for sensitive personal information via email or text message.

Weird payment methods: Is the message asking for a wire transfer? Scam. When money hits the wires, it becomes nearly impossible to get back. Do they want payment through gift cards or cryptocurrency? Also scam. Do they want large stacks of cash in a gym bag? I kid you not, this can happen, especially with home renovation scams.

Urgency: Scams generally try to get the victim to "act now!" Sometimes there's a time-limited offer or date restriction.

Secrecy: Does the message have a warning to "keep matters confidential" and not share the information, winnings, or special-to-you opportunity with anyone else? Very fishy.

Too good to be true: We all want a windfall, but the old adage prevails: If an offer seems too good to be true, it probably is.

Promises of big money and snazzy prizes make useful lures. (This one caught a beloved in-law of mine, now deceased: The scam promised Super Bowl tickets plus travel by private jet for him and three friends, and he so wanted it to be true—even though he was a smart, savvy legal professional. Good-naturedly, he put an actual paper bag over his head for a day as he walked through town, because of course he'd already told everyone his exciting news.)

The other side of this scam are promises to make your debt go away by consolidating it or using a little-known loophole to get out of paying back taxes, credit cards, or other bills.

Bad grammar and spelling: Scammers apparently don't use spell check! Many of these messages originate from other countries, so often the phrasing doesn't appear quite right.

Poor call quality: The caller's voice may have a robotic tone or unnatural rhythm, or your parent may not be able to hear them well due to bad audio quality.

COMMON SCAMS TARGETED AT SENIORS

Government agency scams: Pretending to be agents of the government (typically involved with taxes, criminal justice, or immigration), scammers send out pre-recorded calls or electronic messages. Seniors are likely to be receiving government benefits, so they're common targets. If the scammer already has some data about your parent (such as their age), they will often curate the broader scam to target that information. Scammers typically use official logos (or designs that are reasonably close if you don't have your glasses on) and formal, official-sounding language that nevertheless doesn't quite make sense. These messages also may include threats of legal action, auditing, jail time, or deportation if the victim does not comply.

Financial institution scams: These scams usually come with a nicer-sounding message than the government agency ones. Most commonly, the scammers send fake emails or text messages that look like they're from your parent's bank, asking them to click a link and log into their account. If they do so, their login information is promptly stolen. Some of these fake login portals look obviously dodgy, but more and more (and with the help of good old AI), they're starting to appear worryingly authentic.

Investment scams: With people living longer and consumer costs rising, seniors are more worried than ever before about making their finances last their whole lifetime. Combine that with decades of low interest rates on their savings and promises of high returns with low risks are music to many seniors' ears.

High-pressure tactics, insider information that your parent is supposed to "not tell anyone," Ponzi and pump-and-dump schemes, and good old fake securities are common. Your parent should be especially aware of "affinity fraud" targeted to seniors. This involves scammers wheedling their way into community circles like religious or cultural groups, then telling their "new friends" about a great new investment opportunity. When this scam occurs in seniors' groups, I've heard police ruefully say it's like "shooting fish in a barrel."

Lottery, prize, and inheritance scams: Scammers will try to convince your parent that they have something special with their literal or proverbial name on it—as long as they pay a modest fee and give out some highly personal information. Fancy official-looking documents may be part of this: everything from fake wills or lawyer's letters to equally fake lottery notifications or flyers advertising prize winnings. If your parent pays the fee, there's often another small problem that also requires more funds to be sent—and on and on as long as the scammer figures they can get away with it.

Charity imposter scams: Charity scams are based on asking for donations to a made-up charity or impersonating a real charity. Some involve people "raising money" on the street, holding a clipboard and a donation bucket, or door-to-door collecting, putting up flyers, or advertising on social media. Floods, fires, storm emergencies, pandemics, wartime worries, refugees, sick kids, and suffering animals—you name it. As soon as a real horrible thing is in the news, scammers will whip these up ASAP.

Romance/sweetheart scams: These scams start out as online relationships that the fraudster quickly tires to move to direct text messages or phone calls, creating a greater sense of intimacy and preserving the fake digital identity or another potential victim. Many scammers specifically target seniors' chat rooms, social media platforms, or dating sites.

Usually, after the wooing period, the significant other runs into a conundrum: Their daughter needs surgery, or they need to pay for a plane ticket to go to a funeral in another country. It's usually not a huge amount—well under the ten-thousand-dollar financial scrutiny limit. The scammer may also start asking for personal or financial information, too.

Grandparent scams: This hugely successful scam focuses on a grandparent-grandchild or other family relationship. The phone call almost always starts the same way: The scammer, pretending to be your parent's grandkid, mumbles some confusing phrases asking for help, often saying "grandma" or "grandpa." If your parent tries to figure out who's calling and mentions a kid's name ("Is that you, Paul?"), the scammer latches on and says, "Yes, Grandma, it's me, Paul. I'm in trouble. Don't tell my parents, but I need help."

Typically, Paul needs money because he's in police custody or injured in the hospital. Often, he'll hand the phone over to another person pretending to be a lawyer, police officer, or hospital administrator validating the need for the funds and the method of sending them. This scheme is even more effective because often, the scammer will use sketchy paid "people search" websites to buy as much online personal data as possible and scrape your parent's social media to tailor the conversation.

> ## Security pro tip
>
> Have a family code word that anyone can ask for if they think someone might be impersonating a relative.
>
> "Okay, Paul. I hear that you're in trouble. Can you please tell me the code word?"

As long as this isn't something obvious like your pet's name, the scammer won't be able to guess it. If the impostor "can't remember" the code, your parent should hang up and phone the relative directly. (But watch out—if your parent says they'll call back, the scam artist will probably say that "their" phone was damaged or lost.)

Tech support scams: Older people who may not be as familiar with technology are especially susceptible to these scams. And we all know how often legitimate tech companies ask us to update our software or set up new two-factor authentication, so it can be easy to assume these schemes are real. Typically, scammers pretend to be representatives of big companies like Microsoft, Apple, or Google and include dire warnings about your parent's computer being infected with a virus or, alternatively, needing a free security update. (Oh, the irony.) If the scammer is successful, they'll try to get your parent to give them remote access to their computer, charging them for the service while stealing as much data as possible.

Contractor and home renovation scams: Imagine this: Your parent opens their front door and sees an official-looking contractor in overalls with a labeled clipboard and convincing-looking business cards. (For really thorough home renovation scammers, the business card takes you to a fake website, too. They'll even offer up fake references, with more scammers on the other end of the phone.) It turns out that this contractor was just in the neighborhood doing another job, and they saw that your parent's roof needs some attention. Because they're already working close by, they can offer your parent a special rate as long as they start the project right now. Your parent just needs to pay in cash, with a good chunk of it up front—they should just go to the bank and withdraw what they need. Then the work commences—or rather, the destruction does. This leads to a cycle of more and more money required to fix more and more problems, until one day, the contractor disappears.

> ### Security pro tip
> You or your parent should never hire these "just happened to be in the neighborhood" contractors, no matter how tempting the offer seems. Hire based on referrals from people you know and check out independent online rating sites and the Better Business Bureau.

Strategies for having the conversation

Your parent will know about scams to a certain degree but bringing up a few of these different examples when telling them to be on the lookout can be helpful.

Along with helping them stay informed, you'll want to make sure they feel safe talking to you about any scams that they may still get caught up in anyway. If your parent knows that they've been scammed, they will be embarrassed at best and horrified and broke at worst. If they don't know, getting them to realize what's going on can be even harder.

IF YOU THINK YOUR PARENT HAS BEEN SCAMMED

Before you can take action, you'll need to make sure your parent knows you're on their side and focused on helping rather than judging them. Be reassuring and calm, and don't blame. Your parent will probably be worried that you think they're starting to lose their marbles (and you indeed may be worried about that, but this is definitely not the time to dwell on the issue). Right now, it's your job to be super understanding and keep yourself from saying things like, "Are you serious? You fell for that? Aghh!" That's for your debrief with friends later, but in the moment, you can start with comments more like these:

"Oh, I'm so glad that you told me about this. It was smart of you to let me know. I'm here to help, so let's start figuring out what to do together."

"It can happen to anyone. Heck, I nearly fell for one of these not that long ago."

"Hey, remember that these guys are professionals. And the only reason this fraudster is in business is because he's good at it and his scam works. We'll get it all sorted out."

If your parent hasn't already done so, the first step should be calling the relevant financial institutions to report it—you'll want to notify your parent's bank and credit card companies even if these institutions weren't targeted by the scam. Don't be afraid to do this even if you're not yet 100 percent certain the situation is fraudulent.

You'll also want to help your parent sign up for online credit reporting (this is a pain and can carry a monthly cost, but it's worth it).

Also, make sure your parent changes all their online passwords, not just the account that the scam came from.

IF YOUR PARENT DOESN'T THINK THEY'VE BEEN SCAMMED

In this situation, you have the tough job of untangling what the scammer has done in a way that lets your parent preserve their dignity. You can start by going over an objective list of common scam features, like the ones in this chapter, so they know it's not just their kid worrying over nothing. I'd use the romance/sweetheart scam as an example of red flags to point out, since that type of con can be especially hard to find your way out of—it's not just your parent's money, it's also their boyfriend/girlfriend/online lover/soulmate. Your parent might not immediately rush to thank you for making the scales fall from their eyes, but you can at least get them thinking with a list like this:

- The online object of your parent's affection lives or is traveling outside the country, meaning they can't meet in person.
- They also can't have a video call because the internet is bad, or the cost of data is too high.
- If they do start to make plans to meet, it never actually happens because some disaster always comes up.
- The partner seems almost too good to be true, sweeping your parent off their proverbial feet. They heap flattery on your parent whenever possible.
- The romance is moving fast. Really fast. They quickly take the conversation off whatever site they met on and go directly to text or phone calls.
- There's a lot of contact—the partner showers them with attention throughout the day.
- The partner is having trouble covering unexpected medical or travel costs (or they may need money to come and visit).
- When they ask for funds, they do so through weird money transfers, gift cards, reloadable credit cards you can buy in the gift card section at the grocery store, or cryptocurrency.

Scams are only going to get worse with the increasing popularity of artificial intelligence and greater ability to scour the internet for data. Using code words with relatives, refusing to deal with requests for money except from trusted sources, and regularly learning about the types of scams that are prevalent nowadays are all good ways for your parent to stay on top of the madness. For your part, bring it up, discuss your own and others' experiences with scams, and destigmatize them. Helping your parent feel as comfortable as possible and keeping them alert without making them paranoid are the goals we're aiming for here.

PART 3

Love, loss, and hopefully some laughs

14

How do I cope with all this guilt?

Oh, the guilt that comes with having an aging parent: It can seem never-ending, and there's so much to go around.

Some of this might sound familiar: You feel guilty because you had to get your mother into long-term care. She couldn't keep living independently, but now she's upset and lonely. She wants to "go home," and she's mad and hurt that you "put her in a nursing home"—something she made you promise would never happen. But you couldn't have her living in your condo! There were better long-term care facilities than this one, but it was the only one she could afford. You had to sell her home even though she and your brother loved that house, and your kids loved going there to visit. Now you feel like you're robbing your mother of her home, your brother of his childhood safety blanket, and your children of their special sanctuary with their grandma. Oh, and everyone thinks you're the bad guy, even though no one else is helping.

You're probably not the only one who's feeling like this. Your brother feels guilty because he doesn't live close by and can't help as much. (But, you know, not enough to change his schedule or his golf trips . . .) Your mom feels guilty because she sees you struggling to make ends meet and would like to help out more, but she's so worried about making her pension stretch. She could be worried that you're spending too much time taking care of her, keeping you away from your other family members, relationships, or work.

So. Much. Guilt. (You might even feel guilty about feeling guilty, which is pretty meta—in that case, I can only recommend some light reading on French structuralist philosophy and a stiff shot of whiskey. Let's keep it simple and stick with one plane of existence.)

People often start addressing guilt with a few tried-and-true self-talk scripts. You could give them a go. Though, I can't guarantee they'll work because guilt is complicated.

SELF-TALK #1: EVERYONE HAS GUILT—GET OVER IT!

"Of course you're going to feel guilty. Join the club. But you just have to let that go. Do whatever you need to do to get over it!" (Insert mental backslap and reassuring punch in the arm, plus encouraging head nod. My "stiff upper lip" upbringing would leave the chapter there and be done with it.)

Did that help? No? Well, let's move onto the next one.

SELF-TALK #2: IT'S A PROCESS.

"Working through and making peace with all this is a process. A caregiver support group, friend, counselor, family member, or faith community leader might help. But in the end, know this: The guilt will make you sick, and it won't make anyone else better. So let it go, breathe, and accept."

Maybe that's a bit better? No, not really?

Okay then, it's time to dig deeper and do some of the real work. It will be useful if we first figure out what guilt is, where it comes from, and what it can help us do.

What is guilt?

HOW ACADEMICS DESCRIBE GUILT

"Guilt is an unpleasant emotion implying a *negative self-evaluation against one's moral standards*, that is, the standards concerning those behaviors, goals, beliefs or traits for which one regards oneself as responsible. . . . The wrongdoing can be either actual or potential, that is, a possible consequence of personal traits and dispositions—provided the person views such traits as modifiable through effort (thereby feeling responsible for not trying to modify them). . . . [I]n guilt it is the moral facet of one's self-esteem—the facet concerned with the responsible harmfulness or beneficialness of the self's behavior, attitudes, and dispositions—that suffers a blow."[1]

MY TRANSLATION

Guilt is that bad feeling when either you *already did* something that you shouldn't have, or when you *can't avoid doing* something that you know someone is not going to like. In either case, someone you care about is going to be hurt or mad or both. I typically get it as a sick sensation in my stomach.

Guilt is a weird emotion. As awful as it is to experience, it actually comes from a positive place of morality and "rightdoing." (Yes, that's the actual opposite of "wrongdoing" and not just a word I made up.) Feeling guilt nudges people toward "successful interactions and cooperation within a group."[2] If you feel guilty, it can be a red flag that you should examine a particular situation or action more deeply—think of it as a bit of an emotional divining rod, telling you that something lying beneath needs exploring.

What's guilt trying to tell you?

I'm not saying that every twinge of guilt requires running off to a therapist—although hey, therapy rarely hurts anything except your pocketbook—but guilt should cue you to stop for a moment and really think through what's going on, both on the surface and at deeper levels. Likely there are going to be layers of emotions and history to work though, and that's okay.

If guilt pops up when you're too busy to stop and do an emotional deep-dive at that moment (or that day, or that week . . . the workload of caring for a parent is no joke), you should still make sure to flag it in some way. Send a note to yourself or tell someone around you that this emotion flared when a particular thought or action occurred.

Guilt can sometimes come from a sense of "assumed responsibility" rather than real responsibility for an event or situation. Here's an example.

Real responsibility: "I crashed into my wobbly eighty-nine-year-old grandmother and bumped her down a flight of stairs. She has a broken hip now, and her health is deteriorating. I feel so guilty. I knew she was on the stairs, but she was moving slowly, and I pushed past her, and now she's hurt."

Assumed responsibility: "My seventeen-year-old daughter just crashed into her wobbly eighty-nine-year-old grandmother on a flight of stairs. I know I should have reminded both of them to be careful. Especially my daughter—she's always moving fast. And maybe if I hadn't let my mother go upstairs, this never would have happened." (Insert any other justification, superstition, or fear into that last sentence—"If I had worn my lucky socks, this never would have happened!")

Both situations involve feelings of guilt, but it's important to identify whether that guilt is real or assumed. Just figuring this out might not make you feel any different but getting at the root can help you address the emotions and potentially make changes in the future.

How can I recognize and deal with my guilt?

Before you can do anything about the guilt you feel, you need to figure out where it's really coming from. Ask yourself these questions—it may help if you write them down and answer them in a journal or talk them through with a friend or a professional counselor.

What happened just before I started feeling so guilty? If there are a number of possible triggers, write them all down before deciding if you are feeling guilt about all of them, just a few, or only one. Cross out the things that don't make the cut and let yourself off the emotional hook for those.

What part of it do I actually feel guilty about? Is it the whole decision or situation, or just some of it? For instance, do you feel wholly guilty about putting your mom into long-term care? Or do you mostly feel bad that you broke a promise made years before not to do it? Maybe you're also feeling pretty good about the fact that she will be better looked after in this new situation. In that case, focus on the broken promise and let yourself feel relief about the improved situation.

Did I actually do something wrong, or am I just perceiving that I did something wrong? Dig down into the "real vs. assumed responsibility" debate above. Did you actually take an action that caused harm or pain to someone? Or are you just dealing with a bad situation and drawing those emotions inward to justify other types of pain?

Is someone trying to make me feel guilty? There are all kinds of complicated emotions and dynamics in families with aging parents, especially when time, effort and money are involved.

Try using this process of elimination: If my brother doesn't bring up my decision when we talk, will I still feel so guilty? Yes? Then it's not your brother. What if your sister doesn't give her opinions on your decision? No? Aha. Focus on those interactions with your sister and see what's going on there.

Is there anything I could do to have control over this situation? With this question, you're going to need to pay close attention and be your fully grown-up self, because it can really pull you down old, well-trodden pathways. For instance, you are not in charge of your dad's alcoholism. It is beyond your control—it wasn't in your control when you were five, fifteen, or even thirty-five, and it still isn't when you're fifty-five. It's still his decision, not yours. (PS: You also have no control over your parent's chronic illness, dementia, or mental health issues. Just a friendly reminder.)

How can I stop feeling so guilty?

Yes, here's the payoff you've been waiting for: some action items to help get rid of that horrendous guilt, according to Real Psychologists Who Study These Things.[3]

Communicate. You've been doing all this internal work so far but getting input from the other person or people involved can sometimes show you that your worries are overblown. I can't tell you how many hundreds of times I've talked with an adult child of an aging parent who's turned out to be sick with guilt about something their parent has already reconciled and moved on from. It often sounds like this:

> **Child:** "Mom, I'm so sorry I had to insist you get someone to live with you for home care. I know you never wanted anyone in your house like this. And I know you didn't want to give up your driver's license, either. I hated being a part of ratting you out to the doctor, but there was just no other way. I'm so, so sorry!"
>
> **Parent:** "Oh, I know, darling. But I'm having the best time with my caregiver now, and she drives me all over the place. It's actually been a good change."
>
> **Child:** "Whaaaaaa????"

Set boundaries. If you don't have good boundaries outlining what's okay and what's way too far, you're creating the perfect environment for lots of guilt to grow. To avoid that, set boundaries, share them with others, and stick to them. (Even if you aren't also dealing with a toxic parent, chapter 15 can be a useful resource for learning to flex your boundary-setting skills.) It can sound like this:

> "Yes, Uncle Anil, I see you called again. You've called me six times today while I've been at work. I can't answer personal calls during work hours unless it's an emergency, like if you get hurt or sick. Otherwise, I'll check my messages at 9:00 AM, noon, and 6:00 PM. And I'll call you every other evening around 7:00 or so."

Apologize or try to make amends. On the theme of communication, sometimes just coming out and saying you're sorry helps. It can be hard, but it's very powerful. If you can't speak to the person the guilt is centered on (or if they can't understand you), consider trying to patch things up in another way, whether it's by doing something useful or just writing a letter you don't actually send.

Talk to yourself nicely. Negative self-talk is both mean and counterproductive. There are enough people out there who would be happy to be cruel to you, so don't be one of them. Try to avoid turning "I feel bad about this decision" into "I am a bad person because of this decision."

List all the good things you do. This might sound ridiculous at first but give it a go: Make a list of all the things you're doing for your parent, and if you want, expand it to things you do for your family, friends, community, or (gasp) yourself. Look at that list and realize that when it's weighed against the one thing eating at you, you're generally doing a pretty good job.

Truly understand that you're worthy and have needs, too. Guilt often comes from a place where you're feeling (or being made to feel) that you are self-centered, self-involved, and just plain selfish. You may think that you're not giving enough energy, time, attention, care, or money to something or someone. The best way to prevent this is to build a deep awareness that your needs are worthy and that if your own well is dry, no one else is getting any help from you since you won't have anything to give.

Check up on your mental health. If you're thinking deeply about your guilt and practicing all these solutions yet it's still sticking around, it may be time to talk to a mental health professional. This is especially true if your guilt is starting to manifest in toxic ways (like getting into constant yelling matches with your parent) or leading to compulsive behaviors (like sticking to the same care routine because if you don't, you feel like something bad will happen), depression, or suicidal thoughts. Everyone needs help sometimes, and you need it now.

Forgive yourself because you aren't perfect. This one's pretty self-explanatory. You've probably given this advice to many people over the years, and it's time to remember that this applies to you as well. Sometimes we screw up—it happens. Remember that your intentions matter more than some ideal self you're wishing to be.

Finally, I cannot emphasize enough how important it is to have a supportive group of people around you so that you are not alone in this hard stuff. And don't forget to laugh. Stand-up comedy specials make me chuckle when I think nothing else can—so try to find your own guaranteed source of humor. It helps.

What if my parent is toxic?

None of us like our parents all the time, but some of us might not even be able to stand them. If that's you, you'll probably need to decide what level of emotional connection and financial support you're willing to offer—particularly if there's No One Else™. Managing this complex relationship, figuring out boundaries, and sorting out your legal obligations can be hugely stressful when everyone's not one big happy sitcom family.

Signs it's time to have the conversation

It's also not always easy to figure out *whether* your parent is toxic. If they abused you or your sibling or tossed you out when you were a teenager, that's more clear-cut. But maybe your mom constantly tells you that you'd look better if you lost some weight and left that loser of a partner (whom you adore and have been married to for a decade—but who is a different race than she would have preferred). Or maybe your dad is almost always pleasant to you but loves a nice homophobic "joke" when your partner isn't around.

Overall, you're the one who decides what boundaries work for you. Do you feel like you're always walking on eggshells? Do you often feel like there's no way out of a situation? Do you have to gear yourself up for spending time with them and feel dreadful afterward? Do they revel in spoiling your plans or cutting you down? Then it's probably time to make a change.

Preparing for the conversation

Before we talk about what's best for you, let's figure out a few things about obligations.

AM I REQUIRED TO FINANCIALLY SUPPORT MY PARENT?

Maybe—it depends on the law where you live, so do your research. In many jurisdictions, there are formalized obligations for financial assistance called filial support laws. These laws usually require adult children to only cover necessities, not pay for lavish trips to Caribbean islands. It can be different when there's a profound economic disparity, like a deeply impoverished parent of a profoundly wealthy adult child.

IS MY PARENT OWED A RELATIONSHIP WITH THEIR GRANDCHILDREN?

Let's start here: If your parent abused you and you believe your own child is at risk of abuse, protect your kid. However, if you don't think your kid is in danger, but there's still something in your family that makes the grandkid + parent + grandparent relationship complex, read on.

Legally, there typically aren't "grandparental rights" in the same way there are "parental rights." But some jurisdictions do require parents to support a relationship between grandchildren and grandparents, or at least not actively prevent it.

In terms of your child's well-being, kids with good grandparent relationships get a sense of belonging and comfort as well as improved empathy, social skills, mental resilience, and learning. At the same time, grandparents interacting with grandchildren gain a greater cognitive reserve, verbal fluency, and emotional well-being as well as more physical activity, a sense of purpose, increased empathy, and extended longevity.[1] Both grandkids and grandparents generally benefit from improved mental health and a lower risk of depression.[2]

So overall, there are some upsides to trying to make a tricky situation work. As you figure out what's best for your situation, keep in mind that ideally, this relationship should be separate from your own relationship with your parent. Don't forget that you can ask your kid what they want, too.

You may decide to let your parent interact with your child only while supervised (either by you or by someone you trust). Or maybe you're absolutely confident that your parent will keep their grandchild safe and sound—but you still feel weird about it, maybe jealous or even resentful. That's okay, as long as you don't let those feelings spill over into your interactions with your kid. Adding in a grandchild could even trigger a fresh start for your relationship with your parent (or not, meaning this definitely shouldn't be your main goal).

What if Grandma is rude or otherwise unpleasant to your child, but you still want or need to have your own relationship with your mom? The answers are often practical. Consider not bringing your kid along when you visit your parent or meet at a park so your kid can play while you and your parent chat on a bench. Maybe take separate cars when attending events together.

Strategies for having the conversation

Now, let's talk about what *you* need from your relationship with your parent. Note that toxic parents often react negatively to positive attempts to set good boundaries, but that doesn't mean you should stop trying right away. If you stand firm through the initial absurd adult tantrum, they may get used to these new, healthier ways of doing things.

Map out your boundaries. Make a list of things that you simply won't accept if you're going to continue having a relationship with your parent. Here are a few suggestions.

- A requirement that they call first rather than randomly show up to visit
- Fixed times when visits can happen
- No sharing information about you or your family with others without permission
- No advice about your work, relationships, or general life situation

Accept that they aren't likely to change. I know, this one is hard. But you have control only over what *you* do and say. Hoping your parent will magically change one day isn't practical, so set boundaries for the person they currently are.

Be clear and firm. Use fewer words and explanations than you would in a typical conversation. If your parent tries to take you on a guilt trip to undermine your stance, simply recommit to what you've said. Move the discussion toward specifics—for example, if they say you don't help them out enough, have them say or write down exactly what they need help with.

Refuse to engage in conflict. If you feel emotions ramping up or getting off track, consider making a graceful early exit with a kind excuse.

Be consistent and have consequences. Just like with parenting or animal training, consistency is important. If you say you're going to have a ten-minute call on Sundays as long as your parent doesn't criticize you, then keep that appointment. As soon as they start nitpicking your clothes, hair, and every choice you've made for the past decade, say something like this:

> "Seems like we've wandered into boundary territory. Let's stop now and we can try again next week."

If next week is just as bad, try something like this:

> "It's been a couple of weeks now, but you keep criticizing me. That hurts, and it's out of bounds. I'm going to take a break from our calls and try again in a month or two. Please don't reach out to me until then."

Avoid the weird living room conversation. There's something about sitting down for a "nice chat" with a difficult parent that quickly turns into a living hell. Activities that keep everyone distracted are much better, so if mobility is possible, get moving—go for a walk or push their wheelchair. If it isn't, watch a sports game or a movie together or attend a play or concert. Maybe your thing together is cooking. Just stay out of the living room!

Keep visits short. There's no hard science to back this up, but I've found that frequent ten- or fifteen-minute chats turn out better than two-day visits—probably because you can retreat before anyone has time to get mad. Ninety minutes should be enough for longer visits, since that gives you thirty minutes to get settled into an activity, thirty minutes to do that activity, and thirty minutes to drive back from the activity's location. No matter what, ensure that you have a time scheduled for a "hard out"—you have an appointment to get your nails done or a kid to pick up from softball practice.

Take breaks (including very long ones). No one says you have to have a relationship with your parent. But if you aren't ready to completely cut them off, you can try shorter periods without contact. You can announce it with something like this:

> "I think we're going down a bad road, so let's take a breather for a month or two and we can talk then."

Or you can just be vaguely busy for the next few weeks.

It's impossible to list every single difficulty you might get into with a toxic parent, but here are a few starter scripts that you might tweak to relate to your situation.

> "Dad, I want to talk with you, but when you comment on my weight or my daughter's figure, that's not okay. Don't make judgments about what we—or, frankly, anyone—looks like. If we can agree on that, then I'm happy to keep up our weekly visits. If we can't, then I'm going to stop coming around for a while until something changes. Yes, it's that important to me."

> "Mom, it's not okay for you to speak like that about my spouse. I care for them very much. I also care for you, so I won't let either of you be bullied or insulted. If you keep at it, I'm leaving immediately and won't come back until they get an apology."

"Grandpa, let's agree to disagree on a few things. No more talking about politics, religion, or race relations—we both feel so strongly about those things that we just can't have them in our relationship. There are other, better things to talk about that don't make us so mad."

"Mom, I like sharing things about my life with you, but you tell Aunt Judy and Uncle Rob a lot about me. I'm a private person. Let's assume anything I tell you stays between us unless we agree otherwise."

Why is my parent getting divorced *now*?

Gray divorce is on the rise. When the term was coined decades ago, it mostly referred to the end of a long-term marriage of over thirty years. But it's now become inexorably tied to the Baby Boomer generation: They were the first generation in western society to truly embrace the idea of divorce, and this has not cooled off as they've aged. Today, one out of every four people experiencing divorce is over age fifty. Nearly one in ten is sixty-five or older and that number is increasing.[1] Here are a few reasons why, explained from your parent's point of view.

The empty nester's divorce: "Well, you kids are gone—and frankly, you were the glue that held our relationship together. We've grown apart, and that person across the breakfast table is a stranger now. We've got nothing to talk about and we lead separate lives."

The "I've had it with your habits" divorce: "For forty years, I've put up with your father's addictions, drinking, partying, infidelity, travel, selfishness, softball tournaments, golf obsession, stupid hats, cigars, racist jokes, chewing with his mouth open, and toe fungus. I'm done. I have years left, and I'd rather be alone than with him."

The retirement divorce: "Your dad and I have both retired, and no one goes into the office anymore. Now, he just wanders around the house and gives me annoying advice on how to do things. He's totally lost his sense of self, direction, and purpose. When we retired from work, we realized that we also retired from our relationship."

The ageism divorce (aka the hot girlfriend/boyfriend divorce): "You know your mother . . . well, she's starting to look wrinkled and old, but I'm still young and vital. My yoga instructor is super hot and hip. You'd love her, I'm sure! She's about your age."

The "new me" divorce: "Darling, I'm sick of being in this rut. I'm going to really get into self-improvement. And after I change my wardrobe and mental outlook, I'm going to lose that next 190 pounds—of husband."

The no sex/bad sex divorce: "I know it may pain you to hear about your parents having sex, honey, but we haven't done it in years. I need more and just can't live my life like this any longer."

The lifestyle difference divorce: "What can I say about your father? All he does is yell at the TV in his easy chair."

"What can I say about your mother? She's constantly in motion: at tennis, at charity functions, out backpacking. . . . And it's exhausting—all I want is to be quiet and read a book."

The out of the closet divorce: "I've been living a lie for decades, and I refuse to do it any longer. I'm coming out as a lesbian and taking the next steps forward in living my truth. That means I won't be in this relationship with your dad anymore."

The caregiver divorce: "You know your mother has dementia and she's in care now. She has a hard time speaking and doesn't even recognize me. I care about her, but I can't be married to her any longer because our relationship has developed into caregiving, not a marriage."

(Note: Loving, graceful spouses may divorce the partner with dementia but remain a caregiver.)

The "I fell in love with someone else" divorce (aka infidelity): This story is the same regardless of age. But whether it's the high school reunion or a connection on Facebook, sometimes old flames set things on fire regardless of age.

Signs it's time to have the conversation

Your parents may come right out and tell you that they're thinking of getting a divorce. Maybe they sit you down and have a joint conversation, but the older folks get, the less common this strategy becomes. It will more likely be a one-on-one chat between you and one parent, and while how comfortable this conversation is depends on your family dynamic, I can promise you that it will be emotional and stressful no matter your age.

In some relationships, domestic violence, addiction, and mental health issues can play key roles. These problems may have aged right along with the relationship, or they might be new. While this chapter doesn't delve deeply into those topics, they should be red flags both for gray divorce and elder abuse, and they should prompt you to work on getting your parent psychiatric help or other supports.

VERBAL CUES

If your parent is saying things like, "I'm going to finally do it. I've had enough," or "I just can't take living like this any longer," it may be time to sit them down and start unpacking it. If they are newly, or increasingly, complaining outright or even privately to a confidant that the marriage is just not working, that's a red flag.

PHYSICAL CUES

When you see your parents, are they physically apart from each other? Does one parent turn away from the other, avoid making eye contact, or react with stone-faced repugnance? Is one parent no longer mentally capable of participating in key parts of the relationship like touching, cuddling, or intimacy because of health issues? Changes in physical reactions to each other are warning signs that all may not be well.

SOCIAL CUES

Are your parents driving each other crazy post-retirement now that they're in the same space all the time? Or have they moved on to very separate lives? Does it seem like one of them might be cheating or having another relationship (outside of their relationship rules)? These social changes should make you wonder.

Preparing for the conversation

Gray divorce or separation can be especially hard for many older parents to talk about. There may be shame, fear of losing social standing, or religious barriers, plus overarching worry about what a future apart might look like. This can be particularly true if one partner has more economic or social power.

For others, particularly for those families who have been aware of a bad relationship for years, the talk may revolve more around supporting your parent as they finally get on with it and split up.

Regardless of your situation, consider what you want to achieve. Do you want to empathize and provide emotional support to one or both parties? Do you want to get the issue out on the proverbial table so your parent can stop trying to hide a faltering relationship from their adult kids? Or are you trying to suss out legal and financial problems?

Make a list of your main goals and map out what you're going to say to achieve them. Consider a step-by-step approach in which you don't try to cover more than one category at a time.

Even if the conversation isn't that emotional for you, it likely will be for your parent. Okay, who are we trying to kid? It will probably be emotional for you, too—whether you feel anger, sadness, loss, happiness, or relief that it's finally happening.

Strategies for having the conversation

THE "STRAIGHT TALK" APPROACH

This lacks subtlety, but it can work in some cases: Just sit your parent down and ask them about their relationship straight out. I highly recommend that you do this with each parent individually, since they probably won't feel comfortable having this conversation in front of each other.

"Dad, I wondered if we could talk. I've been thinking about how you and Mom are doing these days. I've noticed that you seem a bit off, maybe even estranged. Can you help me understand how you're feeling?"

THE "OTHER COUPLES" APPROACH

Coming at things a little less directly can give you a bit more room to avoid thorny emotions. With this approach, you bring up someone else's relationship—ideally one of their friends, but if not, then perhaps the parents of someone you know. Try to get your parent to reflect on why they think that couple is splitting up.

"Mom, I heard that your friends the Garcias are splitting up. They're about your age, right? I wonder why they decided to do it now."

Then, try to maneuver your parent toward speculating on relationship issues similar to their own, and see if these second-degree insights help at all.

THE "IT'S OKAY TO LIVE YOUR LIFE" APPROACH

In this case, the parent you're talking to likely falls into one of these categories.

- The caregiver of a spouse with dementia or profound frailty
- The historically maltreated spouse
- The spouse who wants to do things that the other doesn't

Each of these situations is obviously quite different, but they all lead to a conversation that sounds something like this:

"I see and hear how hard this has been on you. Thank you for letting me in. Sometimes change is good, and in this case, I wanted to suggest that maybe things in your relationship could change. We all know that life and love are precious. You've worked hard on this, but maybe you don't need to do that forever. I'm here for you, even if you just want to brainstorm what life could look like outside of this relationship."

THE "HAVE YOU LOST YOUR MIND?" APPROACH

Okay, this strategy isn't for amateurs, and it should be used with profound caution, because there aren't a lot of ways to come back from it. This is the approach you may need to take if your parent *does* run away with that hot young yoga instructor to start up a new, um, reinvigorated lifestyle. I'm not saying that's always uniformly bad—you might be cheering for them—but you can still have misgivings. Be careful: Try to seriously chomp down the emotionally charged words that first come to mind so that you can keep the lines of communication open while still getting your point across.

Instead of actually saying, "WTF, Dad—you look ridiculous with that fake tan, gold chain, and girlfriend who's half your age. Have you finally lost it?" . . . consider something more like:

> "Wow, Dad—I've noticed a big outward change in you. It seems like something huge has happened. Can we sit down so you can debrief me on this a bit? I feel like I'm not up to speed with your life."

Pro tip: You may need to write out a few drafts of a conversational script so you don't explode. Also, make sure you're talking privately in neutral territory where you both feel comfortable— not the family home or the preferred restaurant, but somewhere with a quiet, relaxing atmosphere, like a trail in a local park.

KEY LEGAL AND FINANCIAL PRACTICALITIES TO DISCUSS

After you've started the conversation, there will need to be a time—or more likely many, many times—when you go through the legal and financial practicalities. As long as your parents are mentally capable, it's not actually your place to decide whether the divorce or separation happens. But if it does, you can steer them toward consulting lawyers, accountants, and perhaps mediators. It's important to bring in the relevant experts because if this uncoupling goes badly, it can have far-reaching financial and emotional effects that impact multiple generations.

It's beyond the scope of this guide to go into all the details that need to be worked out during a gray divorce. But broadly speaking, you should talk to your parents (or their divorce lawyers) about the following.

- Financial issues like taxes, capital gains, investments, and pensions
- Spousal or dependent support
- Impact on government program benefits (including veterans' benefits)
- Health, life, and disability insurance
- Ownership of the family home and any vacation properties
- Custody of pets

Lastly, you'll want to discuss changes to your parents' wills and estate planning. If there's a new spouse, what expectations does everyone have about whether that spouse (or their children and grandchildren) will inherit anything? If your family can afford it, talking to a family and estate planning lawyer specializing in gray divorce (also called "later life family law") is absolutely critical. While you're at it, start thinking about whether everyone in the newly forming family units needs to redo their powers of attorney—they probably do. (See the section starting on page 95 for more on powers of attorney.)

No matter what, divorce is hard—even if you've been cheering for one parent to leave the other for years. Counseling and support are very useful and highly recommended for everyone, no matter how old.

Do I have to think about my parent having safe sex?

Okay, relax—this isn't about the intimate details of your parent's sex life. But here's the unfiltered truth: Your parent, like most people, is likely already having, or wants to have, intimate relations and sex. And as you start doing various kinds of caregiving, you might have to acknowledge this.

A study from 2018 found that among seniors ages sixty-five to eighty, 40 percent were sexually active, about half of the men and one-third of the women. It also concluded that sex is important to our overall quality of life as we age.[1] So, whether your parent is continuing to be intimate with their partner, is newly single and ready to jump into the dating pool, or is engaging in some soothing solo sex, let's grit our teeth into a smile and talk about it a little bit. In this chapter, you'll find the good (yay sex!), the bad (boo STIs) and the ugly (tricky consent issues) on safe senior sex.

The good

Sex is fun and makes older people happy. Older people want sex, and older people are having sex. Sex improves quality of life, while a lack of sex makes older people unhappy. Yes, there are honest-to-goodness scientific papers saying all this![2] In fact, sexual satisfaction is a good predictor of what we call "global life satisfaction" in older adults. (If you think you get the drift, feel free to skip the rest of this section.)

Studies often show that frequency of sex and specifically (hold on to your hats) intercourse can be less important than the fact that seniors are engaging in sex at all, in whatever way that's available to them as age and frailty start to interfere. We also know that definitions of what older people consider sex can change too, moving beyond the more traditional (how do I put this elegantly?) copulation.

These many scientific studies are supposed to clinically demonstrate that older people are generally able to find sexual happiness and will redefine sex as part of a gentle reconciliation to the aging process.[3] Personally, and unscientifically, I think these studies all show that people in general tend to like sex and will figure it out as best they can. Because senior sex usually means a pretty broad range of types of intimacy: kissing, cuddling, touching a partner's genitals, penetration, and masturbation.

I know I promised we wouldn't get into the details, but there are two specific topics I'd like to address here.

SOLO SEX

Being older doesn't stop someone from taking matters into their own hands or getting a little battery power. Typically, you wouldn't have to consider this unless you accidentally ran across something you never wanted to see in your mom's Amazon order history. However, if your parent is in a congregate long-term care setting, you may be the one making sure they have all the sex toys and supports they need to truly enjoy later life. One element of this is ensuring that no matter what their living situation looks like, it involves adequate privacy. Going back to Amazon orders, you could also introduce them to the joys of online shopping—lots of choice, zero embarrassment, and tons of useful customer reviews!

LGBTQ+ IDENTITY IN LATER LIFE

Sexual and gender expression have been flourishing thanks to greater acceptance in recent years (finally!), leading to new opportunities for delightful sexual exploration and fulfilling relationships for non-heterosexual older folks. For some, this exploration may be a totally new concept, while for others, it's something that wasn't available or safe for them in their younger years—but now they can start to embrace it.

All this is great, but I also want to raise a few cautionary red flags, too. Some LGBTQ+ older adults, particularly those who are moving into a long-term care facility or some other form of congregate housing, may have fears of entering an environment that's less accepting or includes outright bias. They might worry about having to go back into the closet or conceal their relationships. This is especially true if you're located in places that are increasingly passing laws making it harder for queer and transgender older residents to feel and be safe. Congregate care should be welcoming, and these facilities should have policies in place to support inclusive sexual expression—if they don't, this is both a potential warning sign and an opportunity for you and your parent to work on making a change.

If your parent is part of the LGBTQ+ community, make sure to check on their emotional and sexual safety. See how they're feeling about acceptance, inclusion, and the ability to express themselves. If your parent is experiencing fear, worry, or discrimination, it's probably time for you to escalate these issues to whoever is running their congregate housing—typically the title is something like "director of care."

If you don't get a compassionate answer from your parent's care providers, you may have to go from "polite request" to "raising heck." There are laws and community-based advocacy organizations intended to protect your parent, so seek out the ones in your area. Talk to other families of LGBTQ+ residents, too—finding allies is key. Ultimately, you might have to move your parent to a different facility if you have the means to do so. Do whatever you need to ensure that their well-being, rights, and dignity are being championed.

The bad

There's a good chance your parent is having sex, but there's also a *really* good chance that it isn't particularly safe sex. Their ideas about sexual health may be decades out of date. I can't tell you the number of times I've heard different versions of the following.

"I can't get pregnant."

"He can't get me pregnant."

"He's not gay, so he doesn't have AIDS, and they cured it, anyway."

"We're fine!"

They are definitely *not* fine. And unfortunately, as their adult child, it might be your problem. You really haven't lived until you've reminded your parent about the importance of using a condom. (I wish I was joking, but I'm not.) Right about now, you probably desperately want to skip ahead to the next chapter. Toughen up, buttercup! It's time for extreme dutiful-child obligations.

STIS AND CONDOM USE IN SENIORS

Sexually transmitted infections or STIs (possibly known to your parent by their older name, sexually transmitted diseases or STDs) are rampant in seniors' housing—by the numbers, you would think that some retirement villages are like spring break in 1992. The CDC found that, between 2014 and 2018, among Americans fifty-five and older, cases of gonorrhea rose 164 percent, syphilis 120 percent, and chlamydia 86 percent.[4]

This probably has to do with the fact that people sixty and older use condoms in about 17 percent of their sexual encounters.[5] Why? Firstly, since people are living longer, older adults are getting more chances to have sex with new partners—and if they're widowed or divorced, they may not have had to consider STIs in their previous long-term monogamous relationship.

Here are a few of the many other reasons why older people are often less diligent about safe sex, plus some potential solutions for your parent.

CONDOMS CAN BE HARD TO TALK ABOUT AND EVEN HARDER TO PUT ON

Some older people may just not be familiar with condoms ("Rubbers?" "French letters?") or only have used them for pregnancy concerns, which aren't a big risk for most aging couples. Also, older hands can have a hard time opening the packages and putting condoms on.

There are some assistive technology devices that help people with disabilities put on a condom, but they can be hard to find. Another solution is that if one partner has more dexterity, they could be the one to do the deed. (I know, this is probably making you cringe to consider, let alone bring up. But at the very least, you should be awkwardly asking your parent whether they're using condoms—think of it as revenge for when you started dating your high school crush and they gave you the same talk.)

OLDER WOMEN MAY HAVE HAD LITTLE OR NO SEXUAL EDUCATION

Older women especially can have a more difficult time with sexual health information in general. Depending on their background, they might not have been taught *anything*, including contraception and changes "down there" due to age and menopause.

Of course, things are less stigmatized nowadays, and high-profile healthy-aging champions like Oprah and Michelle Obama are emphasizing the importance of understanding the aging female body. Mentioning that you've heard someone like them talking about sexual health could be a good way to bring up the idea with your parent. And of course, websites for government health organizations and major health care centers have plenty of materials on menopausal or postmenopausal sex and women's health that you might want to print out and leave lying around in some semi-obvious place.

Particularly for older people, gender can be an important factor in the overall awkwardness of discussing sexual health. If you don't think your mom would take very well to you giving her The Talk because you're her son, you could see if your female partner is willing to prove her love to you and start the discussion herself—or maybe you know your dad would do best having this chat with another guy.

HEALTH CARE PROVIDERS RARELY BRING UP SEXUAL HEALTH WITH OLDER PATIENTS

Unfortunately, many family health care providers don't routinely screen for STIs in older patients, or even bring up the topic of sex. Why? Typically, it's ageism, pure and simple. But with STIs increasing as older people embrace their lifelong sexuality more, the generations need to work together to challenge sexual stigma.

If you're the one making your parent's routine medical appointments, consider dropping in an advance request for the doctor to start a discussion about sexual health.

> "Dr. Smith, it's time for my dad's checkup. He's just started dating for the first time since my mom died. When he comes in, can you please have a conversation about safe sex? If he gives you a weird look, maybe tell him it's a routine thing."

The ugly

Our society has come a long way when it comes to sexual consent. Teens learn about it, and college students get regular lectures on the topic. But they weren't running those seminars fifty years ago—or, heck, even twenty or thirty years ago.

Sexual assault can happen at any age and to any gender. Things can get more complicated as people get older, though, because declining mental capacity leads to questions about whether someone can even consent to any form of sex. And some types of cognitive impairment, like dementia, can involve hypersexuality, which can manifest in uncomfortable, unwanted, and occasionally public ways that can be incredibly distressing for everyone.

So, when you're thinking about your parent entering a new relationship (more on that in chapter 19), it's especially important to determine whether one or both parties have cognitive impairment (which you can also learn about in the section starting on page 72). If one person is fully mentally capable and they're having sex with someone who doesn't have the mental capacity to consent, the consequences can range from "having a difficult conversation" to "calling the police."

As always, I'll be focusing on what *you* can do in these situations, but with delicate conversations like these, it's especially useful to consider who would be the best person to deliver the message. It might be you, or it might be a health care professional or a good friend. No matter who gets involved, this may be one of the toughest discussions that will come up in the whole book.

SCENARIO 1

Your dad is mentally capable of consenting to sex, but your mom has pretty profound dementia, so she isn't. However, your dad keeps initiating sex with his wife of forty years.

This needs to be a gentle conversation. Likely, you'll have to go slowly, paying close attention to how your parent is reacting, but the overall topics it should hit sound something like this:

> "I'm so sorry, Dad. We both know Mom isn't the same as she used to be. And I know being both emotionally and physically close to her is really important to you. But she can't consent to having sexual relations anymore—her "yes" doesn't mean the same thing with her dementia. Hand-holding is OK. Even innocent cuddling if she seems to want it. But she can't consent to more, so it's time to let that part of your lives go. I know it's hard. Maybe there's someone we can talk to about this to help you—and everyone—work through how Mom's changes are affecting our lives."

SCENARIO 2

Your mom is in a long-term care home, and Morgan is another resident who lives right next door. Neither Morgan nor your mom are mentally capable of consenting to sex. The two of them keep being found in clearly sexual situations by LTC staff, who always interrupt and redirect them. Your family members who hear about this from the nurses are variously worried, embarrassed, and livid.

In this case, you should speak to your mom's health care provider, and also to Morgan's if they don't share the same doctor. If that doesn't cause the LTC home to take action and stop the situations from happening, you may need to escalate things to the director of care. The conversation could sound something like this:

> "Thanks for meeting with us. I've noticed that Mom and Morgan seem to be very sexually intimate with each other. Our family is worried that our mother doesn't have the mental capacity to consent to sex. We're concerned about a bunch of different things, including the fear that she may be being sexually exploited. If the two of them have a real relationship, let's strategize about how to keep that social or emotional connection going without the sexual element. Maybe either Mom or Morgan could move rooms, so they're kept farther apart. What other strategies do you suggest according to your policies? Let's work together to keep everyone safe, please. This is urgent."

SCENARIO 3

Both of the previous cases involve being certain that one or both of the people involved can't consent to sex, but things get even murkier if your parent has fluctuating mental capacity and you *aren't* sure whether they can consent. In this scenario, let's say your dad has recently been diagnosed with dementia and is now starting a relationship with Chris.

This situation is complicated because depending on how your dad is functioning, he may still be living outside long-term care, perhaps even in his own home. If he's in a place that gives its residents more independence, like in a retirement home or assisted living facility, there are almost certainly some rules around this issue, but in practice, they may be hard to enforce. It's often (relatively) easier in long-term care homes, which typically have explicit policies protecting residents from sexual assault or exploitation—in that case, tweaking the script from Scenario 2 is a good start.

If your dad is in a retirement residence or his own home, you don't get a lot of say in the matter. And you can't exactly pop up in the middle of his special evening, with the wine flowing and Barry White crooning on the sound system, and rapidly administer a mental capacity test—nor can his doctor or psychiatrist. However, you can have a chat where you gently probe into what your dad understands is happening and how he feels about it, which might sound something like this:

> "Dad, I heard that yesterday your friend Chris came over again. Can you tell me a bit about how your visits go? What do you do?"

(Note: Your father may tell you to bug off and get out of his dating life, and he does have a bit of a point.)

Or, if you know more and it's only made you more worried, try something like this:

> "I've noticed that you always seem upset after Chris visits. Can you share a bit about what happens during these visits and how it makes you feel?"

If you do believe that Chris is taking advantage of your dad, his attorney for health and personal care issues may be able to stop Chris from visiting unsupervised or, in some cases, from visiting at all. (To learn more about powers of attorney, see the section starting on page 95.) This doesn't mean that the attorney can make choices about sexual consent for your dad. But if the POA is in effect, it does mean the attorney can make reasonable decisions to keep him safe.

While the attorney may not be legally required to explain the situation to your dad (it can depend on his mental capacity to understand this information and appreciate the consequences), I think it's generally best to be gentle but upfront with him. Your dad may not really comprehend the whole situation but try to tell him what you're worried about in a way he's likely to understand. It might sound something like this:

"Dad, you've said you want to spend time with Chris. I'm worried about what happens to you when Chris comes over, so I'd like to have someone with you for these visits. If I can't be that person, we'll figure out a way to have someone else come along. And if that doesn't work, I'd at least like you to spend time together in a place with other people around, like the park or your favorite restaurant. What's not going to work is having Chris here with you and no one else. OK? Meeting at the café around the corner would be lovely—let's arrange that."

SCENARIO 4

Unfortunately, some cases are quite clear-cut. If a mentally capable staff member or long-term care visitor is found in a sexual situation with your parent, or if another resident is forcing sex on your parent that they obviously don't want, it's your duty to treat this as sexual assault.

Don't hesitate: Call the police and the facility's director of care. You should insist your parent have a medical examination from a team with expertise in both sexual assault of vulnerable people and cognitive impairment. In the case of someone with declining mental capacity who might not fully understand the situation, it's especially important that everyone involved uses the utmost care and gentleness.

After the immediate emergency is over, you should find a therapist for your parent. There are specially trained counselors who work with people who have dementia and have experienced trauma—your local Alzheimer's organization can likely help with finding referrals.

OK, we made it through. If you're still here, give yourself a congratulatory pat on the back and take some time to do something relaxing before reading on. And hey, maybe the rest of the book will all seem easy in comparison (big emphasis on "maybe").

How can I help my grieving parent?

When someone dies, grief takes each of us on a very personal journey, and there's no one "right" way of experiencing the feeling. If your parent loses a spouse quite suddenly, or if the loved one was very dear to them, grieving is likely to hit hard. However, if your mom has been prepared for and reconciled to your dad's eventual death for some time, and your dad is also well and truly ready to pass on at the end of a life well-lived, the immediate grief may be far less. (I'm focusing on your parent's loss of a partner in this chapter because of how common the scenario is, but this advice can also apply to other losses, of course.)

Your family may have "pre-grieved" for a long time, so the partner's passing may happen at the end of the grief process rather than at the beginning. For instance, you may have felt like you were losing a relative with dementia or another terminal illness for several years already. In fact, you and your surviving relatives may be feeling relief rather than grief, and that's okay, too.

Or . . . is there a way to say this nicely? There's a chance you absolutely *loathed* your stepfather, whom your mom stayed with even though he was an abject rotter. And while we don't actually dance on people's graves these days, there may be a little part of you doing a quick shimmy and trying hard not to say things like, "I thought he was too mean to die. Go figure!" In that case, of course you'll need to respect the grief that other people are experiencing and try very, very hard to keep your opinions to yourself. (This is what venting to friends is for. In my opinion, even discussing with siblings or other relatives who've also said they hated him doesn't usually turn out well.) Stick to soothing words and back-rubbing as appropriate.

Folks are often awkward when trying to figure out what to say to someone who has experienced a loss. Rituals of passing can help, and you can ask how your parent or remaining family members think the death should be commemorated.

My best advice? Make sure you open up opportunities to share memories with someone experiencing grief. Ask questions like "When did you know they were the one?" or "What did you love about them?" Invite them to reminisce about past vacations, holidays, and life milestones. If you're up to it, share a story about your own interactions with the person who has passed on.

Here are some other ways to help your parent manage grief.

Be ready for the numbness. Often, after a person dies, there are so many tasks to do that folks stay busy and distracted. Many people will focus on planning the funeral, writing the obituary, or taking care of estate matters instead of their emotional reactions. That's okay—there is no wrong way to feel, and that numbing is a protective way of avoiding overwhelm or falling apart. Don't expect your parent to feel emotional right away.

Acknowledge that emotions will fluctuate, and anger can be real. Similarly, grief doesn't usually express itself in one single, stable emotion. It's more like cycling waves of loneliness, worry, anger, loss, and resignation. We're usually prepared to feel *sad*, but your parent may be outright *mad* at their departed partner. Really, really mad. I can't tell you how many times I've noticed this while speaking with older men who were coping with the loss of a spouse or a close friend. When I got them talking, they admitted that they were furious that the loved one "left them," "deserted them," or that "they just took off."

Denial, anger, bargaining, depression, acceptance. We often talk about the different stages of grief like this, but know that not every emotion always shows up, and it may not happen in that exact order. For some people who have already grieved the long loss of a loved one's well-being to chronic illness, the passing may be quite firmly located in acceptance.

Let everyone grieve in different ways as needed. It sounds obvious, but we often don't carve out time to just sit in grief. It may help to connect with faith or cultural traditions, even if you haven't been particularly observant in the past. Ask your parent what is most important to them about focusing on grief and honoring the life lost.

Find things that create happiness. I'm not suggesting this is the best time to start a major dance party with your parent (although if that's what works for them, go for it). But you should identify small things that bring happiness and do them together. See a movie. Hug a dog. Make a photo album. Rearrange the furniture. Plan a weekend away.

Give help, get help. Like I said before, you should make time to talk with and listen to your parent. There's no perfect thing to say, but being there is always better than potentially making your parent feel abandoned. At the same time, depending on your relationship to the deceased, you'll probably need a listening ear, too—so you can help each other. Of course, don't forget about the option of getting professional help involved. There are also grief groups that get together for group support led by a counselor, and they can even sometimes result in new relationships in the process of working through loss.

There's no one correct way to talk to your parent about grief, so all you can do is your best. And there's no wrong way to experience grief, either. Hold on and be assured that time, love, and new bright spots of activity will bring hope and help.

How do I deal with my parent's new relationship?

T he degree of discomfort and weirdness you feel when your parent starts a new relationship is often based on what their relationship status was before. For instance, if your dad was always single and had raised you solo, you might be understandably protective, even possibly a teeny bit jealous, if he starts dating. Even if your mom lost her husband (your beloved father who could do no wrong) years ago, it can still be hard to get your head around the idea of her moving onto the next romantic phase of her life. And thinking about a new partner moving into the family house you were raised in—or your mom deciding to sell that home and move across the country to be with someone you barely know—can really squeeze your brain.

Let's assume your emotions are going to be mixed at best, presuming you don't actually hate the new romantic partner outright. You could be angry that some upstart is targeting your dad for his money, his house, or his lifestyle (which may or may not be true, and also may not actually matter—his choices are his own). On the bright side, you might be relieved that someone else is now the caregiver for your stepmom. You may also just be happy that your parent is getting out, seeing people, and living life again.

Signs it's time to have the conversation

Ideally, everyone would be mature about this, and your parent would sit you down to have A Talk once they know they've found someone special. But if your parent isn't bringing up the topic themselves, you may have to watch out for signs like the following and consider whether you want to take the initiative and start a chat.

- Your parent starts dodging questions like "What are you doing this weekend?" or "Who are you going to that event with?"

- Your parent spends a lot more time than usual on their phone or online. Text messages are flying in, they're being tagged on social media like Facebook or Instagram, and pictures are showing up that make you go "hmm."

- Your parent starts doing activities with a small group that looks *a lot* like a few couples plus your parent and one other person.

- Your previously-believed-to-be-heterosexual parent starts spending a whole bunch of time with a person of the same gender.

- Your parent shows up at family events with someone new and gives very little explanation as to who they are and what role they're playing in your parent's life.

- Someone gets added to your parent's emergency contact list, power of attorney, will, or other estate planning documents.

- Someone moves into your parent's house. (Seriously . . . sometimes this is actually the first clue.)

But wait, I thought my parent was straight

Just because your parent was in a heterosexual relationship before (say, with your other parent), that doesn't mean they're attracted only to the opposite gender. It's a rainbow world, baby! For many older people, a change in relationship status could offer their first opportunity to explore new types of relationships. This may be totally unexpected for you, but when the scales start falling from your eyes, try not to let them bug out like a cartoon character's. Appropriate comments include, "I'm just glad you're happy" and "Let me know if there's anything I can do to support you." For anything else on the tip of your tongue, such as surprise and confusion? I deeply recommend phoning a friend instead.

Preparing for the conversation

This is one of those times where I'd strongly advise that before talking with your parent, you work through some of your own emotions. If you can do a dry run of the conversation with a therapist or good friend, try that. Depending on how your family functions, you may want to also take a quick temperature check to see how the rest of the relatives are feeling and listen to any worries they might have.

When you're doing your own emotional processing, you might unearth difficult emotions like the following.

- Grief for the loss of your original family unit.

- Concern that the adult kids, including you (the "real family"), will become separated from your parent's "new family." This is especially true if your parent's new partner also brings kids or other dependents into the relationship.

- Worry that the new relationship isn't a "fit" with your existing family or is unseemly in some way (for example, if there's a large age gap).

- Fear that your parent will spend most of their time with the new partner's adult kids and grandkids.

- Judgment that your parent is rushing into a new relationship when their old one has barely ended. I call this "the corpse isn't even cold yet" syndrome, and it seems to happen more with older men. It can be partly denial around the loss, or it can involve feeling dependent on having a partner.

- Concern that your parent may end up having to take care of another partner with health problems, cognitive impairment, or financial issues.

- Worry that your parent is going to get hurt emotionally.

- Fear that your parent is going to be taken advantage of financially.

- Worry that you're going to lose your inheritance, whether that's money or family property like a vacation home.

- Concern that your parent will overshare to you about the new relationship, including all the emotional ups and downs as well as the details of their sex life.

- Discomfort at the thought of your parent being newly sexually active, or not practicing safe sex. Or, frankly, any of it. (See chapter 17 for more help with this, um, delicate issue.)

Here's the thing: I won't tell you that these aren't all pretty valid. I'd say that most of the time, it's a good idea to talk to your parent about their new relationship and bring tough issues like these up, as long as you're in a place in which you can do so tactfully. If that isn't the case, don't rush it, but see what you can do to feel capable of having a productive, empathetic conversation.

Strategies for having the conversation

This is a conversation about your parent and their life, so be prepared to listen. If you feel like you're going to start arguing, consider doing something calming and mildly distracting like repeating a phrase in your head, snapping a hair tie on your wrist, or twirling your pen—whatever helps you avoid interrupting until your parent has said what they want to say.

The first conversation in particular should be an emotional check-in that involves finding out a few facts while being supportive. Of course, that may not be how you actually feel, but it is the persona you'd better put on to start. Once you know more details, you can come back later and have more of a "tough love" discussion.

For now, be gentle and curious. If your parent isn't really opening up about their relationship, or not doing so in a way that allays your worries, remember that getting them to share will take tact and care. Imagine how much *you* probably enjoyed them butting into your teenage (or current!) love life. Recall a time when their comments about your personal judgment cut deeply, even if your parent didn't mean to be hurtful. Then, use that empathy to guide you.

Although gender is complicated and nothing is one-size-fits-all, honest-to-goodness scientific studies have confirmed the old axiom that men talk better "shoulder-to-shoulder" and women talk better "face-to-face."[1] Men can see direct eye contact as challenging, while women can feel that it's important to read their conversational partner's emotions through expressions. If either of those remind you of your parent's personality, you could consider setting up a situation that encourages their preferred type of discussion. Maybe you could bring up the relationship while gardening with your dad or chat with your mom while you're having lunch at your favorite diner.

Here are some openers for both that delicate first conversation and the later talks where you'll dig into the topic more.

THE "FAMILY UPDATE" APPROACH

For an easy, breezy way of bringing your parent's relationship up in a group, integrate an update about their love life into other family updates about kids, jobs, weddings, bat mitzvahs, etc. Slide in something like this:

> "Hey, Uncle Joe, am I right that you're maybe seeing someone new, too? How's that going?"

Then, shut up and listen. Make approving sounds. Let them talk as much as they want, and when it feels like they've said what they want to say, move on to the next update.

THE "HEART-TO-HEART" APPROACH

This is a one-on-one option that uses all your good questioning and listening skills to inquire about your parent's emotions. (Remember: theirs, not yours!) When you talk, reflect back to them what you're hearing them say. Validate their excitement, worry, confusion, caution, or bliss. Remind your parent that you love them and that you want them to be happy. (You know whether this would come across best as a heartfelt comment and hug, or as a casual "love ya" and slap on the back.) If advice or commentary wants to leak out from between your gritted-yet-smiling teeth, chomp down harder, my friend.

THE "I'M CURIOUS" APPROACH

Okay, now it's the second or maybe third time talking with your parent about their new relationship. If things are feeling comfortable, you can start bringing up areas of "curiosity" through open-ended questions. Here are a few examples.

> "I'm curious whether you think that living here and being long-distance is still working for you and Darla. Do you think one of you might move closer to the other someday?"

> "I'm curious about where you see your relationship with Mike going. Does it feel casual, or do you think you've got something serious going on?"

THE "LET'S MAKE A PLAN" APPROACH

By your third conversation, you can probably get away with this more advanced approach. If it looks like your parent's new relationship is going down a long-term path, it might be time to think about getting their estate planning in order. The section on powers of attorney (starting on page 95) has lots of inspiration for starting this type of discussion, but a prompt like the following is often successful.

> "Hey Mom, Pooja and I are getting our estate plans sorted out. Wills, power of attorney, tax stuff, and so on. I'm curious if you're interested in getting in on that, too. I know I'd love your advice on mine, at least. And maybe we can map out what you and your new beau are thinking about in terms of decision-making and wills. Shall we book some time with the lawyer and accountant to work it all though?"

This is a delicate topic, of course, and it can blow up in your face if your parent doesn't welcome you sticking your nose into this type of business. But at the same time, some parents really are very happy to assure their families that they have a new financial and estate plan that *doesn't* blow up everyone's previous expectations, disinherit children and grandchildren, and give the family home to the upstart newcomer (or lovely new person).

THE "WARNING" APPROACH

Sometimes, your parent's new relationship is a disaster in the making. You may recognize their partner as a potential (or current!) abuser. They may be cheating on your parent or treating them badly. Or they may be causing family drama or monopolizing your parent's time.

Immediately trying to convince your parent that their beloved is bad news rarely works, so instead, gently ask how they're feeling about their relationship and if there's anything bothering them. As the conversation goes on, you can eventually mention how you've been trying to visit them or set up plans, but it seems like they've been spending a lot of time with their new girlfriend, and you miss your weekly hangouts.

This almost certainly won't get solved in one conversation, so you'll want to slowly escalate these warnings if you see the bad behavior continuing. Overall, it's important for you to establish yourself as someone safe your parent can come to if they finally get fed up with the relationship. In cases of clear-cut abuse, you'll of course want to prioritize getting your parent out of the situation and involving the authorities if appropriate. But if things fall into a gray area of unpleasantness, you may instead focus on helping your parent maintain their other relationships and safeguard their finances. This could involve talking to a lawyer about setting up specialized trusts, putting some assets out of the reach of the new partner, or getting a cohabitation agreement or prenup. Good luck.

How can I keep my parent connected with the grandkids?

There's nothing better than watching your parent and kids smiling, laughing, and enjoying their time together—but there's also nothing worse than the weird, awkward visit where everyone is sitting uncomfortably in the living room, with the grandkids squirming and the grandparent feeling disconnected. Some relationships between generations are easy, but others need a bit more prompting. If your kids are old enough to talk and do some things on their own, here are a few thoughts about how they can connect with your parent without you in the middle.

Transfer a traditional skill. Does your dad love woodworking? Maybe you have a kid who's all about crafts (or hitting things with hammers) who'd love to get into the work shed with him and learn all about it. Does your great aunt knit like a maniac? Your fashionista teenager could get into making clothes with her help. Gardening, baking a cake, learning to water ski—your parent definitely knows how to do something that your kids would be interested in.

Transfer a digital skill. On the other side of things, your kids could probably teach your parent a lot about the wonders (and horrors?) of technology. Your phone-obsessed child can show Grandma how to text, make videos, use apps, or order things online. The truly brave could sign up for social media accounts or choreograph a TikTok dance together. It might be helpful if you provide a bit of guidance for the teacher here, since, ideally, your parent will be clicking around doing things themselves, with the younger generation providing pointers rather than taking over.

Learn about family history. Most younger people don't have a clue about the names and faces of their extended family. If your kids are curious, they could work together with your parent to do online research and collect the stories and names of people who they otherwise might just know as stiff, unsmiling black-and-white photos on the wall. Using what they've learned, they could create a family tree, scrapbook, or PowerPoint presentation. Grandkids and grandparents can also work together to make themselves part of family history by putting together a time capsule. Tickets and photos from trips, report cards, sports awards, or drawings can all go inside.

Explore cultural events. Your family can set up a regularly recurring "culture night" (or see matinees, which are often better for older people) where the kids go to plays, musicals, or even sports events with their grandparent. Culture can indeed include football or what we call "explosion movies" at our house if your children aren't so into ballet. But beyond building common experiences and creating memories, this could expose your kids to things they don't even know they're interested in yet.

Have a movie/TV night. Maybe the grandkids and grandparents can take turns picking what to watch so that everyone gets to see something new. Getting into a TV show together can be great for recurring hangouts, too. My mothers-in-law took up watching *The X-Files* with my youngest son. I don't really know why, but it became a thing with them, and they still watch it together!

Do puzzles. I confess, I hate puzzles, but I know I'm nearly alone in that. Having something hands-on to do creates a purpose for sitting across or next to each other while chatting, and it gives everyone something to achieve together. I'm always astonished at how well this works.

Play video games. Yes, seriously—your parent can learn Mario Kart. If your kids are into it, Minecraft might be an especially good choice because it allows people to build an online world together that they can come back to again and again. It doesn't matter how good or bad anyone is at the game as long as they're having fun!

Read together. Of course, reading out loud to each other is a classic. But for older kids who might be over being read to, it's equally fun to snuggle up on the couch and page through comics together or enjoy some quiet time while reading separate books.

	Lots more activity ideas
Nature	• Go for a picnic (at a park or in the outdoor area of a long-term care facility). • Take a nature walk. • Go to the beach, lake, or river and swim, dangle feet in the water, sail, paddle, or float around. • Go fishing. • Go geocaching, have a scavenger hunt, or play Pokémon GO. • Visit a playground. • Work in the garden. • Have a bonfire with s'mores and ghost stories.
Culture	• Shop at farmers', antique, or artists' markets. • Visit a museum, either in person or virtually. • Go on an architectural or historical walking tour of the local area. • Hit the amusement park and get on some roller coasters (or watch while the kids do). • Travel together, whether on day trips or longer vacations.
Creativity	• Draw or paint (maybe have everyone work on the same image or theme and compare how they turn out in the end!). • Go to a pottery class. • Take photos or make funny videos. • Write a story together. • Come up with creative mealtime discussion prompts using "conversation starter" boxes or online lists.

	Lots more activity ideas
Food and drink	• Cook or bake together, particularly family or traditional dishes. • Try out new restaurants. • Have a coffee date or tea party. • Taste wine or beer or make cocktails (if your kids are of age!).
Exercise	• Practice a sport together, or have your parent watch or act as a coach. • Sign up for a run or walk benefiting a cause, and even train together if possible. • Play mini golf (this is always hilarious!). • Toss a ball around. • Use a Hula-Hoop (also hilarious—yes, at any age). • Have a dance party.
Games	• Play board and card games—Scrabble, Pictionary, Clue, chess, backgammon, mah-jongg, Go Fish, poker, cribbage, gin rummy. • Try games that get everyone moving—bowling, ping-pong, pool, shuffleboard, cornhole. • Watch a game show and yell out the answers at the TV screen.

In the end, doing almost any fun, age-appropriate activities together will help deepen relationships. Do your best to have something to *do*, and you might start being surprised by how excited your kids are to see their grandparent.

PART 4

Health, hearing issues, and horrible driving

What aging-related medical issues should we watch out for?

Everyone knows that as we get older, things get creakier. Health issues can become more complex, and our ability to bounce back from injuries or illnesses diminishes.

This has been on my mind because I recently got a call from my doctor saying that I now needed (and I'm not kidding) a full physical, bloodwork, an ultrasound, a mammogram, a colonoscopy, a test for hormonal imbalance, and likely a referral to the dreaded endocrinologist to look at my blood sugar. Plus, an updated eye exam, hearing test, and bone density test. "To what," I asked with bugged-out eyes and a heart full of fear, "do I owe this particular terrifying honor? I'm not sick."

"Oh, you turned fifty, so it's time," my doctor said.

"Time for what? Did my warranty somehow expire when I wasn't looking?"

"Well," replied my lovely, long-suffering doctor, "let's review. You've avoided a full physical and internal exam for going on eight years now. You're squinting and have a family history of cataracts. You're leaning toward me and have a family history of hearing loss. You're munching on that delicious-looking muffin and have a family history of diabetes. You also have a family history of colon cancer and osteoarthritis. And it's time to discuss that very special 'change of life' you're going through right now. Have any hot flashes you want to talk about?"

No, I did not want to talk about any of it—and I'm only fifty! But prevention and early identification of symptoms are key, so I dutifully got all my tests done. And, shaken, I started to think a bit more urgently about what else we should keep an eye out for in our parents.

First, we'll go over life-threatening issues, then move onto conditions that are more likely to cause significant disability. For older people, the biggest non-infectious health conditions that can result in death are as follows.

- Heart disease
- Stroke
- Cancer
- Chronic obstructive pulmonary disease (COPD)
- Dementia[1]

Here are quick overviews of each issue (minus dementia, which is handled in depth starting on page 72), including symptoms to look out for and what you need to know before talking with your parent, plus options for doing something about it.

Heart disease

Coronary artery disease (CAD), also called coronary heart disease, is the most common form of heart disease. It occurs when blood vessels that carry blood to the heart become narrowed or blocked, and it can lead to heart attacks.[2]

SYMPTOMS

- Pressure, squeezing, burning, or tightness in the chest during physical activity
- Shortness of breath, especially during physical activity
- Neck, shoulder, or arm pain
- Cold sweats
- Nausea or indigestion
- Dizziness
- Weakness[3]

NOW WHAT?

Medication can address chest pain and/or treat the underlying problems. For folks with a fairly advanced blockage, there are surgeries available.

Stroke

During a stroke, the brain doesn't get enough blood due to a blockage or bleed, leading to brain cell death.

Strokes are always emergencies, so if you suspect your parent is having one, get help right away. The faster a stroke is given medical attention, the better the outcome may be. Unless there's a real reason you can't get emergency transportation, don't drive your parent to the hospital yourself. Instead, call an ambulance because paramedics can attend to your parent with the needed oxygen and other treatment as soon as they arrive.

SYMPTOMS

- Confusion
- Difficulty speaking or understanding speech
- Headache
- Vision troubles in one or both eyes
- Vomiting
- Numbness and/or difficulty moving parts of the face, arm, or leg, particularly on one side of the body
- Trouble walking, including dizziness and/or poor physical coordination[4]

Recognizing a stroke with the FAST protocol

Face drooping: If the person tries to smile, does one side of their face droop?

Arm weakness: If the person tries to raise both their arms, does one arm drift downward?

Speech difficulty: If the person tries to repeat a simple phrase, is their speech slurred or unusual?

Time to act: If you notice any of these symptoms, contact emergency services immediately.[5]

There are differences depending on what type of stroke your parent is having, but on the whole, treatments include medication or surgery.

When emergency services arrive, they will likely push you out of the way and inject something into your parent's arm called tissue plasminogen activator (tPA), which is used to break down blood clots. In general, you have about four hours from the start of your parent's stroke symptoms to get this medication into their body, so time is of the essence.

Surgery to remove a clot using a catheter may also be needed. This must be done within about six hours of the first symptoms.

Post-stroke care varies case by case, but your parent will nearly always require some form of rehabilitation, which might mean physical or speech therapy.[6]

Cancer

Cancer occurs when our bodies produce abnormal cells due to DNA damage and those cells multiply out of control, causing tumors that can potentially spread to other areas. You probably don't need to be told that cancer is horrible. Some forms are survivable, and some aren't, but all are traumatic.

SYMPTOMS

- Lumps, bumps, or skin thickening
- Bladder changes, including trouble urinating or pain or bleeding when urinating
- Bowel changes, such as blood in the stool or changes in bowel habits
- Profound tiredness
- Problems eating, including pain after eating, trouble swallowing, nausea, and vomiting
- Night sweats or fever

- Skin changes, such as moles, freckles, warts, sores that don't heal, too-easy bruising, and changes in skin color
- Unexplained weight gain or loss[7]

NOW WHAT?

Depending on the type of cancer, severity, and spread, the triad of treatments is mostly as follows.

- Surgery to remove the tumor from the body
- Radiation therapy, which uses high doses of radiation to kill cancer cells
- Chemotherapy, which uses drugs to kill cancer cells

Chronic obstructive pulmonary disease (COPD)

If you notice your parent wheezing or having shortness of breath, don't write it off, because it could be COPD.

COPD is a lung condition that makes it hard to breathe, and it's usually caused by emphysema or chronic bronchitis. In turn, those two things typically occur due to smoking. Emphysema damages the air sacs in the lungs, making them no longer able to effectively exchange oxygen and carbon dioxide (or, as I like to call it, *breathe*). Chronic bronchitis involves inflammation of the airway lining that creates and thickens mucus. Bronchitis can sometimes just be a passing sickness, but it becomes "chronic" when it's persistent and resistant to most treatments.

SYMPTOMS

- Shortness of breath during physical activity
- Wheezing
- Chest tightness
- Persistent cough
- For chronic bronchitis, add gross mucus, too

There's no cure for COPD—it's all about managing the condition. Step 1: Stop smoking. Step 2: Don't be around anyone else who's smoking and avoid places with poor air quality.

After that, your parent is likely looking at a future with inhalers, antibiotics when needed, anti-inflammatory medication, supplementary oxygen (often in tanks attached to a tube that is inserted in the nose), and specialized deep-breathing exercises.

Less commonly, they may qualify for some type of surgery. Bullectomies remove some of the big air sacs inhibiting breathing, while lung volume reduction gets rid of damaged tissue. Your parent may also get an endobronchial valve put into the most damaged lung tissue. It's very rare that an older person would qualify for a lung transplant, since age is a key factor in transplant decisions.

Other issues to consider

Right, then—those were the things that kill, but here are the ones that just mess your parent up and cause disability.

- Back and neck pain
- Depressive disorders
- Diabetes
- Falls (see chapter 1 on modifying your parent's home to avoid these)
- Osteoarthritis
- Sensory impairments affecting hearing (see chapter 22), vision (see chapter 23), and touch

Signs it's time to have the conversation

After learning about the symptoms of common conditions, keep an eye out for any of these signs in your parent.

As in my case, another prompt for the conversation is a milestone birthday. If your parent's age ends in "0," it's time for them to get the "your warranty is about to expire" checkup with a battery of proactive diagnostic tests.

Preparing for the conversation

You probably know what your parent is going to say when you suggest medical screening or treatment. Do they hate going to the doctor, like me? Try using guilt or appeals to family medical history. Or do they already consider health screening important? Then just go for reminders. Have a few facts and figures at the ready from this chapter, or from the national organization for whatever condition you're worried about.

Strategies for having the conversation

If you're seeing worrying symptoms but being told it's nothing at all or just a "lingering cold," you can try pulling out the following gambits.

THE "THERE'S AN APP FOR THAT" APPROACH

If you have a smartphone, consider downloading one of the clever apps that provides screening questions or, in some cases, can actually run diagnostics. My phone can already tell me my heart rate and sleep patterns, and with additional apps, it can analyze my coughing, eye health, hearing, and even blood sugar. Once you show off your fancy tech to your parent, you might be able to convince them to download the same app.

> "Hey, check it out! I just figured out how to do a bunch of health monitoring and testing on my phone. Pass me yours and we'll download this stuff there, too. It's amazing what you can do with a smartphone nowadays! Who knew?"
> (Insert innocent blinking if you think you can get away with it.)

THE "QUICK TRIP TO THE PHARMACY" APPROACH

Your parent may not want, or be easily able, to make an appointment with their doctor. However, community pharmacists and walk-in clinics built into pharmacies can be a wonderful source of information, a "quick look" at a symptom, and a trusted person who can sometimes treat or prescribe. Pharmacies may also have some basic easy-to-use diagnostic tools like blood-pressure monitors, which your parent may not mind sticking their arm into while you're waiting in line at the store. You'd be surprised how often a high blood-pressure reading can convince your parent to go to a doctor.

> "Hey Dad, I need to pop over to the pharmacy. I want to ask the pharmacist a few questions and maybe check my blood pressure. Let's go together."

THE "FAMILY AFFAIR" APPROACH

This one is particularly helpful when you have a genetic predisposition toward some condition. Ask your parent if you can talk about family medical histories so that you have information either for yourself or for the grandkids. Based on this discussion, think aloud about what you should get checked out by the doctor. Get your parent to assure you how important this is and how often a person should do that given your family history. Then, ask about where they went to have the screening done and if they recommend their place for things like bloodwork, eye exams, or colonoscopies. Gently probe as to when they last had a test done, and if they're unsure or unwilling to say, see if you can book appointments together.

> "Mom, I'll go and get the eye exam for glaucoma, but let's do it together. If they put those drops in, then we'll both look fabulous in our dark glasses for an afternoon."

What do we do about my parent's hearing problems?

As of 2023, 1.5 billion people globally have hearing loss, and by 2050 that number will increase exponentially to 2.5 billion.[1] About half of folks seventy-five and older have lost thirty-five decibels or more—that's the point when hearing aids are generally prescribed.[2] And yet, hearing loss is widely (and wildly) under-self-reported. In a recent study, only 19 percent of seniors aged seventy to seventy-nine self-reported that they had hearing loss. The actual number? 93 percent—and that number will only go up with age.[3]

That's a lot of hearing loss, so it wouldn't be surprising if this were an issue for your parent. Luckily, hearing aid technology has majorly advanced in recent years, so there's a ready solution.

Think of hearing aids as reading glasses for your ears. In our world of Bluetooth wireless earphones, wireless speakers, closed captioning, and virtual reality, it's odd that there's still such a stigma around the topic. My hope is that this stigma will disappear as the technology improves and costs and barriers decrease—currently, they can be expensive (sometimes five thousand to ten thousand dollars or more) and are often not fully covered by health insurance.[4]

This chapter will discuss some of the practical dos and don'ts of hearing aids, plus other things you can do to support clearer communication with your parent.

Signs it's time to have the conversation

Maybe you're in the car on the way to Nana and Papa's house, reminding your kids to use their BIG VOICES during the visit so Nana can hear them. Or you're trying to watch a movie with your dad while getting your eardrums pummeled because he refuses to have the TV volume any lower than full blast. Either way, you might be starting to suspect that your parent has hearing loss.

Even if it isn't that obvious, check through the following list of indications that it may be time for your parent to have their hearing evaluated. And let's be clear: Even my middle-aged self failed most of these. (Turns out my enthusiastic love of 1980s punk rock concerts did the trick.) So, I'm writing this for you as well as for your parent.

Getting annoyed at "mumblers" or quiet talkers: "Stop mumbling and speak up" is a common complaint. But be careful, as sometimes people (ahem, teens) really do mumble. Actual hearing loss typically starts with missing high-frequency sounds like "ch" and "sh," then other soft consonants follow shortly after.

Difficulty following conversations: Your parent might start smiling and nodding a lot. Or taking breaks or removing themselves from larger discussions. If they lean toward you, it might seem like they're just really interested in the conversation—but nope, they're only registering a smattering of what you're saying.

Here are some other telltale behaviors.

- Cupping their ear
- A fake smile with glassed-over eyes
- Soliloquies (If they ramble on, then their conversational partner is listening rather than speaking. Your parent might tell their story, then immediately leave or mentally check out.)
- Reduced attention
- Turning off the radio when someone talks to them in the car
- Being surprised or jumping when someone talks to them

Not wanting to use the phone: Phones typically use only one ear, which makes it harder to hear. Also, phones don't transmit sound as well as in-person speech does, and your parent can't compensate by reading facial expressions or lips. They may start preferring video calls.

Being startled by loud noises: If your parent sometimes chides you for "yelling" right after struggling to hear you, it's because of something called "recruitment." The hair cells in our ears, which play a central role in our hearing, aren't all lost at the same time, so a sharp or loud noise can still stimulate healthy hair cells to snap to attention. This means that loud sounds become distorted or extra loud.

Struggling with busy, crowded places: Low-grade noise like a fan or the HVAC system can sometimes be tough, but it's often at a lower tone that some folks can more easily tune out. In contrast, trying to listen to just one voice—like your tablemate at dinner—is a struggle when you're competing with all the other people talking nearby at the same level. Your parent may stop attending bigger parties or restaurant get-togethers because not being able to hear keeps them from having fun.

Watching TV too *$@*$# loud: I know, you probably figured that one out on your own. But I cannot tell you how many marriages have been *this* close to breaking up due to excessive TV volume. Dad, let me introduce you to those handy closed captions on the screen and perhaps a nice set of Bluetooth headphones. So much cheaper than divorce!

Becoming awkward or clumsy: Your "inner ear" has two parts: the cochlea, which handles hearing, and the semicircular canals, which deal with balance. They're connected by a fluid-filled space, and so hearing issues can translate into balance issues. Good news: Hearing aids can help with both elements.

Having issues with memory and distraction: If you don't hear a piece of information clearly, it's harder for your brain to process and hold in memory. Plus, it takes a lot of mental energy to focus on absorbing sound and make guesses about what people are saying to fill in the gaps. Does your parent seem zoned out, have short-term memory loss, and look "blank" or "frustrated"? It may be hearing loss rather than the ever-feared dementia, which can be a huge relief.

Preparing for the conversation

Getting ready for this conversation mostly means getting up-to-date about hearing aids. Before we cover the technology, the first thing to know is that they're often an emotional trigger. Hearing aids become the first "big sign" that your parent is getting old and "things are failing." Many older people are upset that they can no longer hear clearly but still refuse to get tested, and some will even deny it.

Vanity and frustration often play a key part in this. Old hearing aids were incredibly ugly—and racist, too, since they were primarily made in light beige skin tones. Even today's hearing aids can be frustrating, because they're small and difficult to keep track of (particularly the new "invisible" ones), and these days they often require a smartphone to use.

To help with all this, let's learn a bit about how hearing aids work, the main types, and how to ensure your parent gets the right features.

HOW HEARING AIDS WORK

Keep in mind: Advancements in hearing aids are proceeding in leaps and bounds, so make sure you're seeking out information that's less than one year old.

Overall, hearing aids help to increase volume, and many make sounds crisper as well. These days, hearing aids are digital, powered by a small battery that either needs to be replaced (this is a pain) or recharged (way better). The digital signals are converted back into sound waves and then delivered into the ear through teeny speakers. New technologies, particularly those using a smartphone app, don't just make sounds louder but can actually analyze and adjust levels to, for example, filter out a person's voice from traffic noise.

Don't let your parent say they'll just get one because they have only one bad ear—all hearing aids require a pair to work.

TYPES OF HEARING AIDS

Type	For	Pros	Cons
Completely in canal (CIC) or mini CIC	Mild to moderate hearing loss	• Molded to ear and usually comfortable • Smallest • Almost invisible • Most people like these • Don't pick up background noise (like wind)	• Use smaller batteries, meaning shorter lifespan • May not have some extra features like volume control, or may require an app • Might not have a directional microphone • Earwax can clog them (eww)
In the canal (ITC)	Mild to moderate hearing loss	• Molded to ear and usually comfortable • A bit bigger, so easier to handle or find if misplaced • Not too visible • Have extra features that the CIC ones don't, like manual volume controls	• Extra features may have such small controls that they're hard to use • Not great with background noise • Earwax can clog them (still eww!)

In the ear (ITE)	All types of hearing loss	• Choice of two styles
		  ○ Full shell (fills the whole ear opening)
		  ○ Half shell (fills only the bottom half of the ear opening)
		• Available with directional microphones (at least two microphones that allow better hearing in noisy environments)
		• Volume control with bigger features
		• Easier to find and harder to lose
		• Typically have a larger battery that lasts longer
			• Might pick up more ambient sounds than smaller hearing aids
			• Easily visible
			• Still with the earwax clogging the speaker!

Type	For	Pros	Cons
Behind the ear (BTE)	All types of hearing loss	• Directional microphones • Loudest • Often have rechargeable batteries • Durable • Less likely to be damaged by moisture and thus last longer • Significantly less earwax!	• Users must be okay with having something behind the ear and a tube going into the ear • The largest type (but getting smaller) • Picks up more wind sounds than other types
Receiver in canal (RIC) or Receiver in ear (RIE)	All types of hearing loss	• Behind-the-ear part is usually smaller than the regular BTE • Directional microphones • Manual controls on the device are fairly easy to use • Usually has rechargeable batteries	• Users must be okay with having something behind the ear and a wire going into the ear • Still visible • Always, always the earwax
Open fit (OF)	Good low-frequency hearing but mild to moderate high-frequency hearing loss	• Naturally allows in low-frequency sounds • User's voice sounds more normal to them, as the whole ear area isn't plugged up	• Pretty darned visible • Often can be uncomfortable • Not usually custom-designed
Over the counter (OTC)	Mild to moderate hearing loss (currently available in the USA)	• Less expensive • No prescription needed	• Not as good as prescription hearing aids (like drugstore reading glasses but for your ears)

Hearing aid features to consider

- Is there a free trial period?
- Is there a warranty? What does it cover?
- How long will they last? (Typically three to seven years.)
- Will someone help set them up and be available for fine-tuning?
- What kind of hearing loss do they help with?
- Are the domes and chargers covered by the price? What about the case?
- Are the batteries rechargeable?
- Do they have directional microphones?
- Is there background noise reduction? How good is it?
- Are they Bluetooth or wireless enabled? (If so, your parent can run their phone, TV, or music directly through their hearing aids.)
- Do they have telecoils? (These can lower background noise and work with older hearing aid–compatible devices like telephones or theater supports.)
- Is there direct audio input using a cord? (This is an older feature.)
- Is there a remote control or an app that turns a phone into a remote control?
- Are there customizable pre-programmed settings? (Like "loud party" or "talking with kids.")
- Do they work both independently and in sync?[5]

HOW MUCH DO HEARING AIDS COST?

There are some great buying resources out there, so you should have a look at consumer reports and guides published by aging or hearing organizations.[6] Before you make a decision, carefully check what their health insurance covers.

Prescription hearing aids can range from one hundred dollars (rare) to ten thousand dollars (a bit on the high side), with the average being about five thousand dollars. To help with the cost, look for specialized assistance programs as well as sales, coupons, and even online discount networks.

Strategies for having the conversation

Even if you use your newfound knowledge of hearing-loss symptoms to convince your parent that there's an issue, they may still resist the solution. If they complain that hearing aids are ugly or ineffective, you can bring out some of the facts about new advancements.

Also, here are two more of the most common arguments against hearing aids you might have to deal with to get your parent to listen. (See what I did there?)

THEIR "IT DOESN'T HURT ANYONE" ARGUMENT

Your parent may claim that their hearing loss doesn't cause any harm, but that's not quite true. Beyond safety issues while walking or driving that can put others in danger, even mild hearing loss takes a toll on the brain. The visual and sensory areas start relying on the auditory cortex to understand sound, causing it to deteriorate over time.

The lack of stimulation to the brain from hearing loss can also cause dementia.[7] (This is usually the argument that wins the day—it's the one that finally convinced my dad to get hearing aids after nearly a lifetime of hearing loss!) With the use of hearing aids, the risk of dementia drops.

You can summarize things like this:

> "Dad, it's less safe for you and for others if you have
> uncorrected hearing loss. You can't hear bells on kids' bikes,
> sirens, smoke detectors, or medical alerts. You can't respond
> to someone in need, like Mom or one of the grandkids, since
> you wouldn't hear their calls for help. And did you know
> that you're also up to three times as likely to fall if you have
> uncorrected hearing loss? So, you really could hurt yourself."[8]

THEIR "IT'S TOO EXPENSIVE" ARGUMENT

If your parent complains about the cost, try something like this:

> "Well, Mom, they can be expensive. But there are a bunch of
> programs that cover the cost, and I'm happy to look into those
> for you. Plus, there are less-expensive products on the market
> that work very well. Also, the costs of not getting them are real,

too. You can't hear your grandkids' voices, you're driving Dad crazy by blasting the TV, and you're at a much greater risk of dementia. So, let's figure out a way to make this work."

NAVIGATING TIME WITH YOUR HARD-OF-HEARING PARENT

If hearing aids don't win the day, you can still use these handy tips to make the time you spend with your parent less frustrating for everyone.

- Don't come up from behind and startle them. Instead, stay in their front range of vision and come in from the side. As you're approaching, gently touch their upper arm to draw their attention.

- Walk up to them rather than calling out to them from another room.

- Meet in quiet, private rooms. No background music, please!

- Look directly at your parent when you're speaking to them.

- If you're explaining something complicated and/or important, provide an easy-to-read document to which they can refer.

- Speak in shorter sentences and pause often to give them time to understand. Ask questions to confirm that they're comprehending.

- Use accessibility tools like flashing lights and vibration on phones and doorbells.

- Use apps like FaceTime or Zoom for video calls rather than calling on the phone. If you are on the phone with them, use a good headset or put the phone directly to your ear to ensure you come across clearly.

- Write things down. Use text messaging or email to share information or confirm details you discussed on the phone.

Hearing loss is incredibly common, but it can also very often be helped. Fear, cost, and stigma can get in the way, but the downsides are even more devastating: cognitive impairment, loss of joy, and disconnection from family and friends. If all else fails, go back to dispelling discomfort by calling hearing aids "reading glasses for your ears."

What do we do about my parent's vision loss?

Vision loss is so common in older age that it often doesn't get the attention it deserves. But from the need for regular eye exams, to the struggles of finding glasses that fit older faces, there's lots to know. In this chapter, we'll talk about common eye-related aging issues, including macular degeneration, glaucoma, and diabetic retinopathy, as well as options and common treatments for your parent.

It isn't exactly news that lots of people need glasses—but for some of us, the changes are slow, and for others they're far more sudden. When I was seventeen, I got an almost laughably light prescription and was delighted because I thought my glasses made me look cool. A week after I turned forty, my glasses "stopped working." When I went to the optometrist, she looked at me indulgently and asked how old I was, then informed me that I had age-related reverse myopia. My prescription reversed itself—I'd gone from not being able to see far away to not being able to see close up. I didn't even know that was a thing! Then, almost a week after I turned fifty, those cute light-prescription reading glasses with a nearly non-existent astigmatism correction also started to get "foggy." I went back to the same optometrist, and she started talking about progressive lenses and bifocals.

All this to say, eyes change, whether it's due to strain, aging, disease, or other conditions. So, here are some things to look out for. (Eh? The puns just keep getting better, don't they?)

Signs it's time to have the conversation

If your parent is sixty-five or older, they need annual eye exams. Easy.

Signs of vision deterioration can show up as behaviors that you might initially brush off as old-timer personality quirks, or they might be easier to recognize as physical issues. If you notice several of these clues appearing out of nowhere, you should encourage your parent to visit the eye doctor to find out the cause.

Behaviors	Physical symptoms
• Holding written text (like restaurant menus) up to their nose • Squinting to read signs • Preferring to go to the movies rather than the theater or opera (where there's a small stage farther away) • Choosing bright over dull-colored objects or clothing • Not wanting to drive at night, or making driving mistakes in general • Becoming clumsy (for example, spilling food or having trouble threading a needle) • Falling because of a missed step or an unseen object on the floor • Getting startled when you approach them from the side • Not noticing objects in the middle of their vision • Struggling to recognize faces • Having visual hallucinations • Keeping the lighting in their home very bright, or conversely, getting overwhelmed by normal lighting that they say is "too bright"	• Headaches or eye strain (which can cause them to massage their head or put pressure on their "sore eyes" with hands or a cold cloth) • Nausea or vomiting • Red or clouded eyes • Uncontrolled eye movements • Frequent changes in eyeglass or contact lens prescription

Preparing for the conversation

If you suspect something might be wrong with your parent's vision, you'll want to learn a bit about the main types of aging-related eye problems and see if any seem familiar. This chapter gets a bit technical, so I've heavily referenced materials from the Mayo Clinic, which does a great job of explaining everything.

NEARSIGHTEDNESS (MYOPIA)

Medical explanation

For people with normal vision, images are sharply focused onto the part of their eye called the retina. But for nearsighted people, the point of focus is in front of the retina, which makes distant objects appear blurry. Glasses or contact lenses optically correct the problem by altering the way the image enters the eye, but they don't cure myopia.[1]

Risk factors

Myopia can be hereditary, or it might occur spontaneously. It can be associated with long periods of activities that require close-up vision (like reading or screen use) and a lack of time spent outdoors.

What it really means

This is a fancy way to say, "You can't see far away." Your parent might have had this issue for years, but it could be getting worse.

If untreated, myopia can impact your parent's ability to drive, ride a bike, or see oncoming traffic as a pedestrian. It can also lead to worries about becoming lost in places like stores, since they might not be able to read the aisle markers.

Now what?

Simple enough—your parent will need an eye exam plus new glasses or contacts. Less commonly, refractive surgery is required.

GLAUCOMA

Medical explanation

Glaucoma develops when pressure in the eye starts to destroy the nerve fibers in the retina. This pressure usually comes from a build-up of fluid in the front part of the eye. In normal amounts, this fluid nourishes the eye and keeps it inflated, but issues with creating or draining the liquid can lead to problematic imbalances.[2]

Risk factors

- Family history
- Black, Asian, or Hispanic heritage
- Diabetes, heart disease, high blood pressure, or sickle cell anemia
- Extreme near- or farsightedness
- Previous eye injury or surgery
- Long-standing use of corticosteroid medications, especially eye drops

What it really means

Glaucoma will make your parent's peripheral vision really bad, although they may not notice it until their field of vision becomes very narrow. It usually shows up in both eyes, but it could begin in just one. It can also eventually cause blindness, so it's something to take seriously—even with treatment, about 15 percent of people with glaucoma become blind in at least one eye within twenty years.[3]

Now what?

The goal with glaucoma is reducing the buildup of fluid pressure in the eye, and it's typically treated with medication and possibly laser or conventional eye surgery. Surgery can stop the problem from getting worse, but it can't reverse vision loss, and it may need to be repeated, since the results can be temporary. More rarely, an eye drain can be inserted.[4]

AGE-RELATED MACULAR DEGENERATION (AMD)

Medical explanation

Macular degeneration occurs when the macula (the central part of the retina responsible for sharp focus) is damaged, causing permanent central vision loss.

There are two different yet related types: dry and wet. About 80 percent of people get the dry form. With dry AMD, the macula gets thinner with age and tiny clumps of protein called drusen grow. The wet form is more serious, since it leads to faster vision loss. It occurs when abnormal blood vessels grow under the retina and leak fluids that cause scarring of the macula. Dry and wet AMD are treated differently, so you should find out which kind your parent is diagnosed with.

Risk factors

- Family history
- White heritage
- Obesity
- Cardiovascular disease
- Tobacco use[5]

What it really means

Macular degeneration will cause your parent to slowly lose their central vision, meaning that everything will get really blurry until they pretty much can't see. You'll want to pay careful attention to make sure your parent doesn't become socially isolated or depressed, since these are common side effects.

Now what?

Regular eye exams can detect the disease early on—and it's important to catch it quickly, since laser treatments can slow down the vision loss.[6] New injection treatments are also very promising, and for wet AMD, medication can be used as well.

Your parent will likely get regular eye injections, which can be costly depending on your location and health care coverage. Your lives may start to focus on the timing of these eye injections—they typically occur around four to five weeks apart.

If your parent isn't tech-savvy, you can teach them about podcasts, audiobooks, and other non-visual reading formats that will be better for their new limitations. When you interact with them, try standing slightly to their left or right while they look straight ahead so you stay outside the blurry spot in their vision. (Yes, this will probably feel weird at first.)

CATARACTS

Medical explanation

Cataracts are cloudy areas in the eye's lens. They occur because, as people age, the lenses in their eyes become less flexible, less transparent, and thicker. At the same time, proteins and fibers in the lenses break down and then come together in cloudy clumps that stop light from reaching the retina.

Cataracts aren't a disease, just a natural aging-related process. They generally develop in both eyes, but they don't always form at the same rate, so the level of vision loss can be different in each eye.[7]

Risk factors

Beyond aging, cataracts can be caused by too much exposure to UV rays due to being outside a lot without wearing good-quality sunglasses. They can also be an unfortunate side effect of some medications, like corticosteroids.

What it really means

Your parent is simply getting old, and so are their eyes! Cataracts generally grow slowly, and in the earlier stages, they likely aren't going to be too bothersome. As they progress, your parent may have trouble recognizing faces and figuring out expressions. Driving at night will eventually go from hard to inadvisable to downright dangerous.

Now what?

Your parent should probably get stronger eyeglasses, plus some fab new UV-rated sunglasses. They will also need brighter light to see properly, so turn on some lamps when you're spending time together. Overall, they can slow down cataract development with boring old "eating right and exercising."

When these solutions stop working, it's off to a routine laser surgery known as a capsulotomy—but everyone pretty much just calls it "cataract surgery" (or, my personal favorite, "getting your eyes zapped"). Once the surgery is done, they'll regain their ability to drive safely, work on precise tasks, and use a computer without discomfort. Sometimes cataracts do return after surgery, requiring more surgical intervention later.

RETINAL DIABETES

Medical explanation

Yep—this is a problem with the retina that's linked to having diabetes. I always appreciate it when the medical community actually names things helpfully!

Medically, what's actually happening here is that changes to blood vessels caused by diabetes deprive the retina of oxygen. This can cause deteriorating eyesight and, eventually, blindness.

The following are the two types of diabetic retinopathy.[8]

- **Early diabetic retinopathy, or nonproliferative diabetic retinopathy (NPDR):** In this more common form, new blood vessels stop growing in the retina. At the same time, the walls of old blood vessels weaken, causing bulging as well as leakage of fluid and blood.

- **Advanced diabetic retinopathy, or proliferative diabetic retinopathy (PDR):** As PDR progresses, the damaged blood vessels can start to close themselves off, causing new, abnormal vessels to grow in the retina. These new vessels are fragile and can leak into the clear, jellylike substance that fills the center of the eye, making pressure build in the eyeball. This buildup can damage the optic nerve that carries images from the eye to the brain and result in glaucoma. Scar tissue from the growth of new blood vessels can even eventually cause the retina to detach from the back of the eye.

Risk factors

Anyone who has diabetes can develop diabetic retinopathy, but the following features can make it more likely.

- Black, Hispanic, or Native American heritage
- Longer history of diabetes
- Poor blood-sugar management
- High blood pressure or cholesterol
- Pregnancy
- Tobacco use

What it really means

As I explained oh-so-disgustingly above, retinopathy leaves your parent at risk of glaucoma, retinal detachment, and even complete vision loss if the condition is poorly managed. You'll want to make sure they get to an eye specialist as soon as possible.

Now what?

This may sound obvious, but please, get your parent to tell their eye specialist that they're diabetic and specify type 1 or 2 so the specialist can look for the right markers.

This matters because early treatment can be quite successful in slowing down or stopping vision loss. Your parent might get the following interventions.

- **Vascular endothelial growth factor inhibitors (VEGFs):** Medications injected into the eye to stop new blood vessel growth and decrease fluid buildup.

- **Photocoagulation:** A laser treatment that can stop or slow leakage of blood and fluid.

- **Panretinal photocoagulation:** Another laser treatment that can shrink abnormal blood vessels.

- **Vitrectomy:** A surgery involving making a tiny incision in the eye to remove blood and scar tissue that are pulling on the retina.

Unfortunately, none of these treatments can cure diabetic retinopathy—because diabetes is a lifelong condition, future retinal damage and vision loss are still possible, and often still likely.

Vision is so important and new advancements in this area are made every day. If you take away only one thing from this chapter, it should be this: Make sure your parent gets checked annually!

What do we do about my parent's incontinence?

Oh, yes: The joys of toileting. I promise that your parent hates this even more than you do.

This chapter both explores key issues related to incontinence and provides some often-unexplored aids for regaining continence. It will also teach you to support your parent while you're out together, whether you're shopping, exercising, or at the theater. (Disclaimer: There will be poop jokes. I can't help it—either it's my way of coping, or I have the sense of humor of a nine-year-old.)

Signs it's time to take action

Your parent might be dealing with incontinence if they demonstrate the following behaviors.

- Won't attend long events with seats jammed together, like movies, plays, concerts, or religious services
- Refuse beverages
- Won't go out for walks far from home or to unknown areas
- No longer want to go on car trips longer than twenty or thirty minutes
- Worry about air travel more than they used to, maybe wanting an aisle seat near the back of the plane
- End up regularly seeing the doctor for repeated urinary tract infections (UTIs)

Preparing to take action

#1: LET'S START WITH URINARY INCONTINENCE (UI)[1]

The following are the three main types of UI.

- **Stress incontinence** is the classic "I laughed so hard I peed my pants" version: involuntary leakage of urine that happens with exertion like sneezing or laughing. Any pregnant woman can tell you about this one. It's less prevalent for men, but it does happen.

- **Urge incontinence** is involuntary leakage of urine that occurs right after feeling a sudden urge to urinate. People with overactive bladders sometimes experience this. If you've ever had a UTI, had to chug a gallon of water before an ultrasound, or been holiday shopping with a toddler in a busy mall where you can't find a bathroom, you know this awful feeling.

- **Mixed incontinence** is involuntary leakage of urine that combines stress and urge incontinence.

  The following are a few additional subtypes of UI.

- **Incontinence associated with retention of urine** (also known as overflow incontinence) is leakage that occurs when the bladder doesn't empty completely. You know when you think you're done peeing, but then you aren't? That.

- **Functional incontinence** is leakage that occurs because of the inability to get to the toilet. This includes conditions like arthritis and mobility issues that make bending, undoing clothing, or positioning one's body difficult.

- **Continuous incontinence** is constant leakage. This is associated with numerous medical conditions.

UI is a common problem, but it's tough to get accurate statistics, since the issue can be awkward for people to discuss. Around the world, between 25 and 45 percent of women and between 1 and 39 percent of men report dealing with it.[2] Beyond aging, conditions like menopause, diabetes, hypertension, obesity, prostate problems, neurological conditions, and dementia can all be contributing factors.

If your parent deals with UI, it's unfortunately very likely to have a significant effect on their life: 41 percent of people describe their leakage as problematic, and 40 percent report embarrassment around their condition.[3]

#2: THE REAL POOP ON FECAL INCONTINENCE (FI)

Fecal incontinence (sometimes called bowel incontinence) can range from the occasional leakage while passing gas (okay, admit it, it's happened to all of us) to a complete loss of bowel control. (Think along the lines of your really bad choice to have dinner at the local seaside shack that one time.) Gas and bloating are also often part of the whole FI experience.

If FI occurs temporarily during an occasional bout of diarrhea, that's not something to worry about—chronic or recurring FI is the real problem. The following are the two types.

- **Urge incontinence** is an inability to stop a sudden urge to poop.
- **Passive incontinence** is caused by not being aware of the urge to poop at all.

It's important to accurately diagnose the type of incontinence your parent has because treatments are different for each.

Common causes include diarrhea, constipation, and muscle or nerve damage.[4] I know that's essentially saying, "having poop issues can make you poop a lot," but there are many specific problems that can lead to FI, including diabetes, hyperthyroidism, irritable bowel syndrome (IBS), Crohn's disease, colitis, and trouble absorbing certain nutrients (also called malabsorption). A much simpler source may be medication issues—is your parent taking their meds with food when they should be taking them on an empty stomach, or vice versa? Have they started a new medication or changed their dosage?[5]

Strategies for taking action

It's important to get your parent to the doctor first, since as you just read, incontinence can be caused by all kinds of medical issues—and there are medications and other treatments that can help. But besides that obvious step, here are some other tips you can help your parent implement.

THINGS TO AVOID OR REDUCE

Urinary Incontinence[6]	Fecal Incontinence[7]	Both

• Any food or drink that acts as a diuretic, including
  ○ artificial sweeteners
  ○ carbonated drinks
  ○ chocolate
  ○ chile peppers
  ○ foods that are high in spice, sugar, or acid, especially citrus fruits
• Certain medications: heart and blood pressure meds, sedatives, and muscle relaxers
• Smoking (to decrease coughing)
• Vitamin C in large doses
	• Foods that your parent is allergic or sensitive to (now's not a bad time to check for new allergies)
	• Certain vegetables: nightshades like tomatoes, or veggies that produce more gas like cabbage and broccoli
	• Overuse or misuse of laxatives
	• Running (no, really—watch out for runner's diarrhea!)
		• Alcohol
		• Caffeine
		• Dairy

PEE- AND POO-PROOF FASHION

Clothing that helps with incontinence has been getting much better in recent years—and it's about damn time! Mainstream brands that cater to both women and men are producing "period panties" or "moisture control" underwear that give a real sense of comfort, elegance, and normalcy.

However, these undies work best for small, episodic amounts of leakage. For heavier-duty products, you'll want to look for pads and liners. Pads attach to underwear just like period pads—the ones with "wings" that adhere to the sides as well as the bottom are especially useful. Liners tend to be thinner, wider, and longer, since they're designed to protect "front to back."

Many old-style pads and liners have a waterproof backing that stops any leakage into the rest of the clothing. Newer versions have a "breathable" plastic film, which I recommend, since it's much better at reducing skin irritation and a lot more comfortable. If you're looking to be eco-friendly, some versions are washable and reusable.

For men, there are incontinence products specifically created that help in the area where they often need that extra dryness. New wicking material is becoming trendy for men's shorts, pants, and underwear, but there is still a bias toward these products being more available for women (since they are often created to help with menstruation, too.)

If pads and liners aren't enough, adult diapers are your solution. They also come in both disposable and reusable versions (although, I confess, I prefer disposable). Some are "pull-ups" that can be put on just like underwear, and others have adhesive tabs that make the fit more precise.

If you're the one buying, do your research and look at a bunch of different products, touching them to see how they feel, if possible. Even if you're leading the mission, take your parent along if you can. Remember, style and appearance can really matter, and preserving dignity and personal choice is important.

KEEPING IT CLEAN

Disposable and washable products each create their own challenges. Disposable is all about the smell and general ickiness. Remember the diaper pails we used for babies? They make adult versions. Likewise, for washable products, follow the same procedure as you would for babies' diapers: Empty the poop first, consider soaking them in a bucket or sink with a laundry product, and then wash them.

In general, baking soda is helpful for smells. You can purchase other urine neutralizers at the hardware store. Top tip: If you can't find what you're looking for, check out the pet section, since those neutralizers for furniture or carpet work just as well and may cost less.

When it comes to wiping, toilet paper may not cut it for some older folks. Adult wipes can be helpful, and there are all sorts of varieties whose advertising sounds like you're getting a trip to a fancy spa: "organic" and "alcohol-free" and "aloe vera–enhanced." Pay attention to whether or not they're flushable, and make sure your parent can open the package easily.

PROTECTION AROUND THE HOUSE

"Pee pads" is a terrible name for the first useful item on my list, but you've probably seen them before—likely in hospitals or if you've done any pet or toddler toilet training. They're usually blue and plastic-y on one side with a white cotton liner on the other, and they come in different sizes. They're disposable, highly absorbent, not too expensive, and easy to find in most grocery stores (and they're often even cheaper at pet stores or big-box stores). There are also eco-friendly washable flannel versions you can consider. Whatever type you choose, you can set them up on furniture around the house or pop them into a handbag for use while out and about.

A protective mattress or sofa cover is probably best for your parent's bed, couch, or favorite chair. You may want to put down a protective sheet or pad. (Yep, these are pretty much the same thing used for kids during potty training.) I've found better versions searching the internet than going to the store. Try to avoid the ones that feel especially like plastic, since they are less comfortable.

If you have more money to spend on this, you can also consider switching to vinyl or other kinds of easily wipeable furniture. Cloth couches and chairs are the worst for staining, and leather is better but still not great. Luckily, we've come a long way from ugly retro vinyl loungers, so there's no need to sacrifice design for a wipeable surface.

HANDLING ACCIDENTS

Being prepared with the things you need to clean and change, plus the right attitude, is key to dealing with accidents gracefully. If you're feeling frustrated, remember that your parent hates the situation more than you do (or, if they are no longer mentally capable of sharing that information with you, I think it's fair to say that they're at least more uncomfortable). But yeah, parent poop is gross. But just like with kid poop and dog poop, you get used to it.

You can create a "go bag" to carry outside the house with extra clothes, products, and wipes, plus a washcloth, a towel, some soap, and a perfume of choice if you're feeling fancy.

When it happens, be empathetic and try phrases like these:

"Mom, shall we pop over to the bathroom? I think we can both freshen up there."

"Oops, I'm sorry about the accident. Nothing to worry about—it happens to lots of people. Let's just go get this sorted."

"That's one of the joys of life. You should have seen me after my kids!"

25

———

Does my parent have issues with alcohol?

I can't tell you the number of times I've heard versions of "I love my dad, but not after three o'clock in the afternoon. You can't call after three." And increasingly, I'm hearing, "My mom never really used to drink, but since she retired and hasn't been doing much, she's hitting the cocktails harder and harder." Or, "Since his partner died, he's been drowning his sorrows."

There are lots of reasons why people might start drinking more as they age, as well as a bunch of really good reasons why they shouldn't do this. Aging bodies often can't handle alcohol well: It increases the risk of high blood pressure, cancer, and just about every other unwanted health complication. It can make an older person unsteady, reduce the effectiveness of their medications, mess up their memory, cause issues with their digestion ... and damage their relationships.[1] Lots of people drink despite the risks, so there's no judgment here—I just want to help you help your parent take care of their health.

If your parent has always been a drinker, it's unfortunately unlikely that you'll be able to change them easily now. In fact, the likelihood of someone altering their very well-established drinking habits decreases the older they get (although it certainly can be done with treatment and motivation).[2] And let's not forget that changing cultural norms can make things tougher. My father's dad was a "man of the north," which translated into a number of positive things, but also a lifetime of really awful whiskey and roll-your-own cigarettes. By today's standards, his behaviors were both deeply unhealthy and surrounded by waving red flags labeled "addiction." But for when and where he lived, he was just a regular guy. I say all this not to depress you, but to keep your expectations realistic as you consider working on this issue.

Signs it's time to have the conversation

If you're uncertain about whether your parent's drinking has become an issue, start by comparing their behaviors against this list of red flags for "problematic" drinking. Does your parent demonstrate any of the following behaviors?[3]

- Say they "can't stop" drinking or get anxious at suggestions that they stop
- Say that they should cut down on drinking without ever following through
- Make excuses for drinking or make up stories to cover up their habits
- Withdraw from relationships and social activities
- Neglect personal hygiene and housework
- Have problems with sleep
- Have an "eye opener" drink to wake up in the morning
- Hide drinks in unusual vessels (like whiskey in a teacup or wine in a coffee mug) or conceal bottles around the house
- Regularly act irritable, depressed, or confused (including slurred speech)
- Struggle with a lack of coordination or falls
- Have stomach problems (including lack of desire to eat)

Preparing for the conversation

If that list was relatable, you'll want to take action. You'll also want to consider how your parent's drinking might affect their mental capacity. (For more about mental capacity, see the section starting on page 72.) The irony is that your parent's capacity to make good decisions about drinking is actually impaired by their drinking, creating a circular problem.

Most worryingly, alcohol and alcoholism can cause or increase your parent's risk of some forms of dementia. There's even a condition called Wernicke-Korsakoff syndrome that's commonly known as alcohol-related dementia, although it's actually a separate condition. Like dementia, it can cause forgetfulness, anger, confusion, and lashing out.[4]

But even beyond those more serious issues, alcohol can really mess with your parent's brain. Here's some of the science associated with mental capacity, alcohol, and aging, plus my translations of what it really means.

In the words of the experts:

"The [brain's] frontal cortex controls executive function, and the prefrontal area has prominent projections to the basal ganglia and amygdala, controlling impulsivity and compulsivity. Disruption of this frontal cortex control is part of the causative mechanism of AUD [alcohol use disorder]."[5]

My translation:

If your older parent drinks too much alcohol, decision-making will get harder for them. Alcohol quite literally hurts their brain and keeps them from thinking straight.

In the words of the experts:

"Particularly with alcohol, the negative emotional states associated with aging may converge with the negative emotional states of alcohol withdrawal, which drives many individuals with AUD to self-medicate to avoid experiencing negative effects. . . . This convergence, in turn, could also drive the need to self-medicate. In short, alcohol misuse in the elderly population may tap into misdirected attempts at emotional self-regulation, in which an individual consumes alcohol to fix the problem that alcohol helped cause."[6]

My translation:

If your parent is already unhappy about the physical effects of old age, trying to drink less and add alcohol withdrawal onto those issues can feel overwhelming. To cope with these stressors, your parent might drink more to make themselves feel better, because addiction is definitely not big on logic.

In the words of the experts:

"Many medicines—including prescription, over-the-counter, or herbal remedies—can be dangerous or even deadly when mixed with alcohol. A lot of older people take medications every day and are more likely to take one or more medications that interact with alcohol, increasing their risk for harmful alcohol–medication interactions."[7]

My translation:

Aunt Kiri—your groovy herbal concoctions that you think are so *healthy* could literally kill you when combined with a couple of martinis and your blood pressure meds. You can keep taking the herbal concoctions, but let's focus on the martinis, shall we?

All this would stress anyone out. But if you were a child of an alcoholic parent, it's especially important to assess how you're feeling, since some painful old patterns are probably coming back (if they left at all). Do any of the following statements resonate with you?

- "I swear to [insert deity of choice], if I have to hear him slur his words one more time, I'm going to start smashing things."
- "You know what? It's her choice. She can go ahead and drink herself to death."
- "If they cared about their kids as much as they cared about Chardonnay, they'd have been Parent of the Year every single year."
- "Hell no, I'm not leaving my kids with Grandma. Especially after cocktail hour."
- "It's fine." (Obvious note: When someone says this, it's almost *never* fine.)

If you've identified that your parent's problematic drinking is triggering you, congrats—no, really. Awareness helps. Once you know there's an issue, you can be more intentional about caring for yourself, too, which might involve seeing a therapist or finding community support like Al-Anon's family groups.

Strategies for having the conversation

Okay, so you've judged the problem's severity, its potential impact on mental capacity, and your own responses. But how do you address it?

THE "STRAIGHT TALK" APPROACH

As always, if you think your parent will be open to it, a clear and straightforward conversation is the way to go. However, this approach requires your parent to be in a mental state where they can clear-headedly address the issue, plus you have a strong enough relationship to withstand any potential defensiveness.

> "Mom, I'm really worried about your drinking and how the alcohol is affecting you. I'd like to talk with you about it."

THE "MAKES IT WORSE" APPROACH

If your parent has health issues such as diabetes, pain, dizziness, heart issues, infections, or problems with blood pressure, alcohol can really make things worse. In some cases, the consequences will be direct: For instance, alcohol can immediately affect diabetics' blood sugar. In other cases, it's more subtle: Alcohol decreases the effectiveness of many antibiotics, for example, and it can compound the side effects of pain medication, causing confusion, grogginess, and instability.

Come at this with the intention of genuinely educating your parent about something they may not know. But keep in mind, if your parent is alcohol-dependent, this may cause them to avoid taking their meds or become more secretive about their drinking.

> "Dad, can we talk a bit about how alcohol affects your blood pressure? I know it can make some medications less effective—we should check to see if that applies to yours."

THE "ASK YOUR DOCTOR" APPROACH

Relatedly, you can suggest that your parent bring up the effects of alcohol at their next medical appointment. If you'll be at the appointment too, you can ask how much and how often it is safe.

If your parent trusts their doctor, they can be a voice of authority where you've failed. Even if your parent doesn't end up listening, this approach at least puts the issue on the medical professional's radar. However, if this backfires, your parent may become angry or defensive, or even stop wanting to visit that particular doctor.

> "Dr. Chan, I've been reading about how drinking affects different people at different ages. Can you tell us how much alcohol would be okay for someone my dad's age with his medical conditions?"

THE "LET'S GET HELP" APPROACH

This is my favorite approach, especially for parents who have been dealing with problematic drinking for a longer time, and particularly for children who have their own trauma around a parent's alcoholism. It's safe and effective—but it does carry a risk of backlash if your parent refuses to admit that the issue has reached this level.

Detoxing an older person should be done by skilled professionals using evidence-based strategies, which may include harm reduction (working toward fewer negative consequences from your parent's drinking, without requiring them to stop altogether), group therapy, cognitive behavioral therapy, or even rehab. But before you get there, you'll need to convince your parent to reach out.

> "Dad, I think it's time we got some help for your drinking. I know this isn't your fault, and I support you. Let's reach out together and find someone who knows what they're doing."

THE "SNEAKY" APPROACH

This is only for the most desperate situations and shouldn't be used if your parent is in fact alcohol-dependent, as it can cause serious withdrawal symptoms. But if your parent needs to cut down on drinking for their health and doesn't have the mental capacity to make that decision themselves, it may be the way to go.

With this approach, you don't say anything to your parent, but you do start mixing non-alcoholic spirits into the alcoholic version to reduce its potency. (Yes, you can buy non-alcoholic rum, gin, vodka, whiskey, beer, and many more these days, and some of it is even pretty good.) If this works, it's a harm-reduction strategy that allows your parent to enjoy a drink with less impact on their well-being.

How this conversation goes is likely going to be based on how aware your parent is about their issues with alcohol, and how long-standing the problem has been. No matter what you say, do your best to keep any blame out of your voice, because no one wins the blame game. "It's a problem. It's an addiction. It's an illness. It's not their fault." Chanting this to yourself a few thousand times might help. Harm reduction will be key, and even if it doesn't get you exactly where you want to be, it's worth trying.

How can we manage my parent's medications?

On average, older North Americans take between five and six daily medications, and in some regions, the number is as high as eight or nine.[1] In some western countries, 25 percent of seniors are prescribed ten or more drug classes at the same time.[2] Not drugs—*classes* of drugs. Layering in vitamins, supplements, over-the-counter medications, and homeopathic remedies gets us into the double digits pretty fast, and also pretty deeply dopey.

This (over?)use of many medications simultaneously is called *polypharmacy*. (Casually drop that term into a conversation with your parent's health care provider and prepare to see them look impressed.) The thing is, even medications that are absolutely necessary can interact, creating problems or sometimes even canceling each other out. So, it's incredibly important for you and your parent to stay on top of everything they're taking, including the non-prescription stuff.

Signs you need to take action

If you notice your parent demonstrating any of the following behaviors, it's time to figure out what's going on and work with them and their doctor to make a new medication plan.

Behaviors	Symptoms

• Skipping doses
• Taking larger doses than prescribed
• Failing to fill prescriptions
• Leaving expired meds sitting around
• Continuing to use old medications even though the health issue they were meant to treat has gotten better already
• Starting to take lots of new homeopathic, naturopathic, or over-the-counter medications
• Forgetting to eat (or not eat, depending on the type of medication) before taking meds
	• No improvement in the health issue the medication is prescribed to treat
	• Unexplained new health issues, such as
	  ○ mood changes
	  ○ sleep changes
	  ○ rashes

Preparing to take action

Go through the following steps one by one (with whatever level of parental involvement makes sense for your parent's mental capacity) before reaching out to a medical professional.

ASSUME YOUR PARENT IS LYING ABOUT THEIR MEDS

Whoa—I know. If you don't like to think they are "lying," you can reframe this as "not providing you with absolutely accurate information." Why do I know they're lying about their meds? Because everyone does it in conversations like this:

Health care provider: Do you take all your medications every day as prescribed?

What your parent says: Sure I do.

What your parent thinks: Usually. Most days. I don't like those big ones for pain because they make me constipated, and I feel fine even if I don't take them every day. Also, I can't take those blue ones with alcohol and sometimes I'd like a little cocktail. I don't always get all my prescriptions filled at the same time, so I do occasionally run out. Some of the meds I'm supposed to take on an empty stomach and the others I'm supposed to take on a full stomach, so it's fifty-fifty which instruction I follow.

Health care provider: And do you take them at the right time and in the proper amounts?

What your parent says: Oh, *absolutely.* You can't mess around with medications. I'm never late with them, and I never skip them, either—that's dangerous!

What your parent thinks: I totally mess around with medications. I'm really not a morning person, so sometimes I sleep through the time when I'm supposed to take my morning meds. I usually just make it up by taking the morning dose in the early afternoon, and then a few hours later, I take the evening dose. And well, sometimes I need to stretch out my medications because they're expensive, so I cut my pills in half to make them last through the month. Or on days when the pain gets bad, I double up on that dosage.

Health care provider: Do you dispose of expired medications properly?

What your parent says: Always.

What your parent thinks: Never. I might need them again someday, and then I won't even have the trouble of going to the doctor. Those opioids I got after my dental surgery? Keeping those bad boys. And everyone knows that expiration dates aren't really a thing. I've got canned tuna from 1999 that's still good.

Like I said, everyone does this a bit (I can't confirm or deny how many of the examples are relevant to my own life). I've created this imaginary conversation not to encourage you to accuse your parent of something they might not have done, but to remind you to pay attention to what you can see in your parent's behavior and medicine cabinet as much as what they tell you.

GATHER UP ALL YOUR PARENT'S MEDICATIONS

This next step involves a trip to the medicine cabinet. You'll want to locate all your parent's prescribed meds, supplements, health powders, vitamins, special juices with pain relievers of all kinds, tonics, tinctures, suspicious packets of dried herbs stored in the closet, topical creams, and anything else you can think of.

Start with the traditional medicine cabinet, but also search all bathroom cupboards and drawers. Then check out the kitchen—there's nearly always a stash of old (probably expired) meds somewhere in there, usually in the junk drawer or the cabinet above the stove, so get on that step stool, push aside that never-used silver polish, and dig around. Don't forget the fridge, especially the fridge door.

If your parent carries a handbag, tote bag, or backpack, go through those, too—all of them. Finally, if your parent drives, check their car's console and glove box, plus between the seats.

Beware of grapefruit

While you're excavating your parent's house, consider tossing out any grapefruit or grapefruit juice. When it comes to medication, that stuff's nothing but trouble. Many medications are metabolized with the help of a vital enzyme called CYP3A4, but grapefruit can block this enzyme's action. Then, instead of being metabolized, more of the drug enters the blood and sticks around longer, resulting in way too much of the medication in the body.[3] It sounds far-fetched, but this is a real problem!

MAKE A MEDICATION LIST

Once you have all the meds lined up, take photos of everything (both the outside label and the actual medication itself). For pills or gel tabs, the shape, color, and engraving or other written information are identifiers. For liquids, you can note the color and thickness.

Then, create a photo album, both on your phone and as a hard copy. You can also use this chart as a starting point for a written list. Give copies to your parent and make them available to health care providers, who will be both grateful and deeply impressed.

Your parent's medication list	
Prescription	
Over-the-counter (OTC)	
Occasional use (e.g., stool softeners)	
Vitamins and supplements	
Alternative medicines (e.g., traditional Chinese medicine)	
Topical creams (e.g., antifungal creams)	
Recreational drugs or alcohol (frequency and type)	
Other	

Strategies for taking action

Now, let's look at what should be done during and after the big appointment.

SCHEDULE A MEDICATION REVIEW

In a medication review appointment, your parent goes over each item in their regimen with a professional. Often, the best person to do this with is a pharmacist rather than a doctor, as your parent's various doctors are likely to focus on the drugs related to their own specialties rather than see the overall picture. If you don't already have a relationship with a pharmacist, get a recommendation from someone you trust.

GO TO THE MEDICATION REVIEW

Bring all medications, current and expired (and everything else on your list), to the appointment. I usually create multiple Ziplock bags with meds grouped according to the sections in the chart above. If there's anything you can't take along, your phone pictures are your backup.

The health care provider may or may not try to hug you out of gratitude—they're used to either getting a deluge of random junk emptied onto their desk or being presented with a single prescription pill, neither of which are very helpful.

Also, bring yourself. It's important to try really hard to be present because you'll be an extra set of ears who can also helpfully take notes. There's usually a lot of information flying by that can be confusing for any one person alone. If it's allowed, you could record the appointment to replay later and/or keep as a record if you're acting as your parent's attorney for health and personal care decisions.

STAY ORGANIZED

Once you've figured out your parent's medication regimen, you'll want to help them set up their new schedule of responsible medication management. (I'm being very optimistic here, yes.)

Of course, if your parent doesn't already have them, you can purchase medication dispensers and pill organizers. Nowadays, some high-tech versions can display notifications or even give verbal reminders (which I find both helpful and slightly creepy).

If your parent has trouble keeping track of doses when their meds come loose in a bottle, ask if the pharmacy can fill the prescription in a blister pack or pre-created pill organizer. These are genius, I swear.

SET UP REMINDERS

In addition, smart speakers like Google Home or Amazon Alexa can be programmed to give medication reminders—and automatically send refill requests. Depending on how annoying (or funny) your parent might find this, you could set up a message from you to play at certain times of day, like this:

"Hey Dad, it's your favorite daughter! It's time for your yellow blood pressure pills. They're in the pill box by the bathroom sink. Let me know when you've taken them!"

Top 5 medication mistakes

1. Skipping meds or taking them at the wrong time of day
2. Taking the wrong dosage
3. Accidentally doubling a dosage after forgetting that the meds were already taken
4. Taking OTC meds that interact with a prescription
5. Not paying attention to food interactions

BE VIGILANT ABOUT STREET DRUGS AND ADDICTION

Cannabis, opioids, Valium—we've got all of them and more in our senior population. Why? The Baby Boomer generation is aging, and this age group has had a very different relationship with drugs than their predecessors. Plus, the increasing availability and legalization of drugs like psychedelics has led to a significantly reduced stigma. Just like anyone else, older adults use drugs for purposes like fun or pain management and may have long-standing addictions.

Problematic drug use is going to be one of those things you can't even begin to solve alone as an adult child, so this is where I simply remind you that there are geriatric addiction assistance programs. However, I also never want you to assume that your parent couldn't possibly be using or misusing drugs.

If this is an issue in your family, a great starting resource is *Not As Prescribed*, a book published by the AARP and written by Dr. Harry Haroutunian, the former Physician Director of Professional and Residential Programs at the Hazelden Betty Ford Center for drug and alcohol treatment. It goes more deeply into medication management (including how to do a medication review) and has great explanations for how we think about, avoid, and rationalize addiction in aging.

Is it time for my parent to stop driving?

"Taking away the keys" is one of the most hated topics, and one without perfect solutions for most people. Imagine this: You're pretty sure your dad shouldn't be driving. He's lost his peripheral vision and can't see well in the dark anymore, and you're more nervous sitting in his passenger seat than you are with your sixteen-year-old. But can you really tell him to get out from behind the wheel?

This chapter will discuss options, since it isn't always an all-or-nothing decision. Dad may end up voluntarily choosing not to drive at night or on major highways. He might get a new car that's easier for him to drive, or you could work together to find him alternative transit options. Regardless, there are insurance and liability questions, plus maybe a guest appearance from the family doctor.

There's a lot at stake here, because you aren't just worried about your dad getting into an accident and hurting himself. You can acknowledge that this is a risk he's willing to take—but poor driving is a serious risk to others, too. But here are some reassuring facts for you: Older drivers tend to wear their seatbelts, and as long as they're fit to drive, they're the least likely age group to be involved in collisions or kill pedestrians and cyclists.[1]

And as usual, we can find some humor in the situation. Just look at the case of my beloved childhood doctor, a true pillar of the community. The story goes that before her driving days ended, she ran her car right through the plate-glass window of the local fish shop. With the vehicle now firmly lodged inside the shop, she got out, brushed off the glass, and ordered the night's halibut. No one was hurt, so we can laugh about it now, but we still want to keep your parent from entering their neighborhood businesses by any method except for the door.

Signs it's time to have the conversation

Close calls: Your parent tells a lot of "funny" stories that involve nearly hitting another car, person, or object. Or, if you're unlucky, you're in the car beside them for these incidents. Friends and family members might talk to you about how worried your parent's driving makes them.

Bumps and scrapes: There are new marks on your parent's car, or on their driveway fences, garage, lawn, or curb. Their driveway markers or standalone mailboxes have been knocked over.

Honking and yelling: While there's always inappropriate road rage, your parent gets called out by other drivers or pedestrians much more often than usual. Your parent might also have an unusually strong emotional response to these callouts, or they may seem to not notice and show no reaction at all.

Tickets, warnings, or cautions: Your parent is getting unusual traffic tickets or police warnings. (Note the "unusual"—I'm not talking about the rare speeding ticket for going fifty in a forty-five zone.)

Getting lost: Your parent gets confused on the way to familiar locations like the grocery store or bank.

Trouble following road cues: Your parent has difficulty noticing traffic signals or reading road signs and markings.

Delayed responses: Your parent has trouble moving their foot from the gas pedal to the brake, or issues changing gears. Or they have difficulty turning their head to check over their shoulder while merging, changing lanes, or backing up.

Time and space misjudgment: Your parent struggles to figure out how much time they need to merge in and out of traffic. They stomp on the brakes instead of easing into slowdowns.

Lack of concentration: Your parent has a hard time focusing while driving. They might take their eyes off the road or take their hands off the wheel to gesticulate while talking. Even worse, they could completely forget that they're driving.

Preparing for the conversation

KNOW YOUR OPTIONS

Like I said before, the outcomes aren't only "car keys or no car keys." You might want to set a goal for your discussion that involves self-regulation, where your parent chooses to take steps to reduce their driving risk. Your goal could be for your parent to do the following.

- Drive only short distances to and from places they know well.
- Drive only in quiet local areas with low traffic flow (no highways).
- Drive only in the daytime (not in the evening or at night).
- Drive only in good weather (no rain, fog, or snow).
- Downsize to a smaller car.
- Get a car with safety features (like backup cameras, collision warning sensors, automatic parking assistance, or merge control).

Most people don't know this, but there are also a host of courses and other resources available to help older people sharpen their driving skills. Some private driving instructors specialize in helping senior drivers, and advocacy organizations or insurance companies offer online programs.

And finally, don't forget about the wonders of technology. Rideshare apps like Uber and Lyft can be wonderful alternatives to driving, especially in cities where they're more common. You can pitch it to your parent by emphasizing that they won't get stuck in traffic and there are now no parking challenges, and all the while they'll feel "with it," since these apps are used by all ages. Money doesn't change hands, and the account can be hooked up to a credit card to deal with charges automatically. You can even set up a family account.

BUT IF THE LICENSE DOES NEED TO GO AWAY . . .

The process of licensing, retesting, and license revocation is a bit different depending on where you live, but most jurisdictions have license renewal requirements for older people. Drivers may also have to go through driving or health evaluations by licensing agencies based on observations from police, doctors, family members, or even personnel at licensing offices. Other policies for further testing include vision screening, road tests, knowledge tests, and evaluations by medical advisory boards.

I often hear the complaint, "Why can't my parent's doctor just take their license away?" Often, doctors can do this—but usually they don't *want* to, since this could make your parent so angry that they never come back to their office! And some medical professionals simply believe that this isn't their job. Also, doctors can remove or suspend a license only if they have a solid reason, like your parent suffers from seizures, vision loss, or there are findings on a mental capacity assessment that specifically relate to driving.

Strategies for having the conversation

Since most of us can't rely on the family doctor to save us from this awkward situation, here are some other methods to consider.

THE "SUBTLE" APPROACH

When you're spending time with your parent, bring up your car every now and then. Complain about the terrible roads and traffic and ask how your parent is managing. Propose hypothetical scenarios: If they didn't absolutely have to drive, would they still want to? In this way, you'll learn about their needs and habits as well as what driving means to them. Store that information away and use it to help you follow through with some of these other approaches.

THE "STRAIGHT TALK" APPROACH

If you're lucky, your parent might be very matter-of-fact about the topic, so you can bring it up without any sugarcoating.

> "Dad, I'm worried about your driving as you get older. We need a plan in case you can't do it in the future. What are your thoughts?"

If your parent agrees that they're having some challenges, start problem-solving together using what you learned in the previous section.

THE "FAMILY MEETING" APPROACH

Get everyone in your family who lives nearby and is of driving age together for a chat over snacks. Each person should talk about how they're managing their transportation and what they would do if they couldn't drive or get a ride from their usual source. You can bring up all kinds of scenarios: disaster preparedness, backup plans in case someone breaks their foot, or how to get the kids to sports practice when everyone's so busy lately. By the end, everyone should have a plan in case of emergency—and from there, you can start getting your parent more comfortable with putting that plan into action sooner rather than later.

THE "SELF-REFERENTIAL" APPROACH

This is a bit like the previous approach, but with a one-on-one conversation.

Tell your parent that you've been thinking about what you would do if you couldn't drive. If you have any life circumstances that might make this possible someday (like a medical condition or prescription), you can use that as justification. Walk through different scenarios: How would you do the grocery shopping? How would you visit family and friends in different cities?

Then ask your parent what going without a car would be like for them. Was there ever a time where they couldn't drive and didn't have anyone to help them with transportation? Ask for their input on your hypothetical situation and get them to walk you through what kind of help you could give them in theirs.

THE "DRIVER'S LICENSE RENEWAL" APPROACH

If your parent's mandatory license renewal is coming up and you're worried they might fail (and believe they really shouldn't be driving), the problem might get solved for you. If you go to the appointment with them, you could use some underhanded strategies: Chat with the person behind the counter and make a knowing comment or two about how it's a "great idea to get testing done, especially since their eyeglass prescription has really changed lately," plus a significant eyebrow raise. If they fail, they fail.

THE "NUCLEAR" APPROACH

Sometimes, none of the gentler strategies will work. Driving is key to your parent's happiness and self-image—they love to drive, love their car, and will never willingly give up—but they've got medical concerns like dementia or terrible eyesight. In this case, you really will have to convince a health care provider to write a note for driving cessation and give notice to your parent's auto insurer.

WHEN NOTHING ELSE WORKS

If the nuclear approach has come into play and your parent keeps driving illegally, you can dip into these last-resort ideas. I want to be clear: I don't advocate for "tricking" anyone, so I'll just tell you what some folks do when they're very concerned about safety and leave it at that.

- Leave the car in the driveway but hide the keys.
- Replace the real keys with keys that don't fit the car.
- Take out the key fob's battery.

- Let the car's battery drain down so it won't start.

- Remove something vital from the car, like the alternator.

- Take the car away to get it "fixed." Maybe it will be "in the shop" for a long time.

- Ask your parent to "lend" the car to a grandkid.

- Sell the car (*only* if you have legal authority to do so—see the section on powers of attorney starting on page 95).

Regardless of which approach you take, you should absolutely prepare yourself to do something—for everyone's safety. Your parent may be more receptive to a "stepped" approach, where they stop driving at night first, then reduce highway driving later, and so on. Tread gently but firmly on this topic.

Conclusion

No one needs to remind *anyone* that families are tough, and parent-child relationships of any vintage are complex at all ages.

I'm hoping that this book has been something that you can read, share, laugh with, yell at, and delve deeply into for real information about how to make it through these difficult years without losing your head or your relationships.

We often assume that we'll have time to deal with these issues over the gentle course of years or even decades. The reality is that the timeline may actually be quite short and compressed. And I don't know which way is better. What I do know is that it's hard. It's sometimes hilarious. It's often frustrating. But I hope this helps.

LTW

Notes

Chapter 1

1. Joanne Binette and Fanni Farago, *2021 Home and Community Preference Survey: A National Survey of Adults Age 18-Plus* (Washington, DC: AARP Research, November 2021), https://doi.org/10.26419/res.00479.001.

National Institute on Ageing and Environics Institute for Survey Research, *Perspectives on Growing Older in Canada: The 2022 NIA Ageing in Canada Survey* (Toronto: National Institute on Ageing, Toronto Metropolitan University, December 2022), https://www.environicsinstitute.org/docs/default-source/project-documents/nia-2022-ageing-in-canada-survey/2022-survey-report---perspectives-on-growing-older-in-canada.pdf.

2. Jonathan Vespa, Jeremy Engelberg, and Wan He, *Old Housing, New Needs: Are U.S. Homes Ready for an Aging Population?* (Washington, DC: US Census Bureau, May 2020), census.gov/library/publications/2020/demo/p23-217.html.

3. Age Safe America is one example. I'm not endorsing them—just using them as an example of a provider who does this type of work: https://agesafeamerica.com/senior-home-safety.

4. Simran Mundi et al., "Similar mortality rates in hip fracture patients over the past 31 years," *Acta Orthopaedica* 85, no. 1 (February 2014): 54–9, https://doi.org/10.3109/17453674.2013.878831.

5. J. Negrete-Corona, J. C. Alvarado-Soriano, and L. A. Reyes-Santiago, "Hip fracture as risk factor for mortality in patients over 65 years of age. Case-control study," *Acta Ortopédica Mexicana* 28, no. 6 (November–December 2014): 352–62. https://pubmed.ncbi.nlm.nih.gov/26016287.

6. Kristina A. Theis et al., "Prevalence of Arthritis and Arthritis-Attributable Activity Limitation—United States, 2016–2018," *Morbidity and Mortality Weekly Report* 70, no. 40 (October 2021): 1401–7, http://dx.doi.org/10.15585/mmwr.mm7040a2.

Chapter 2

1. AARP and National Alliance for Caregiving, *Caregiving in the United States 2020* (Washington, DC: AARP, May 2020), https://doi.org/10.26419/ppi.00103.001.

Canadian Centre for Caregiving Excellence, *Giving Care: An Approach to a Better Caregiving Landscape in Canada* (Toronto: Canadian Centre for Caregiving Excellence, November 2022), https://canadiancaregiving.org/wp-content/uploads/2022/11/ccce_giving-care.pdf.

2. United Nations Department of Economic and Social Affairs, *The Growing Need for Long-Term Care* (New York: United Nations, August 2016), https://www.un.org/esa/socdev/ageing/documents/un-ageing_briefing-paper_long-term-care.pdf.

Organisation for Economic Co-Operation and Development, *Long-Term Care Resources and Utilisation* (Paris: OECD, July 2023), "Long-term care recipients," https://stats.oecd.org/index.aspx?datasetcode=health_ltcr.

Chapter 5

1. "Facts & Figures," American Health Care Association and National Center for Assisted Living (AHCA/NCAL), accessed April 28, 2021, https://www.ahcancal.org/assisted-living/facts-and-figures/pages/default.aspx.

"Living Arrangements of Seniors," 2011 Census of Population, Statistics Canada, last modified July 23, 2018, https://www12.statcan.gc.ca/census-recensement/2011/as-sa/98-312-x/98-312-x2011003_4-eng.cfm.

"Deciding When It's Time," Ontario Retirement Communities Association, accessed September 27, 2023, https://www.orcaretirement.com/retirement-living/deciding-when-its-time.

2. "Facts & Figures," American Health Care Association and National Center for Assisted Living (AHCA/NCAL), accessed April 28, 2021, https://www.ahcancal.org/assisted-living/facts-and-figures/pages/default.aspx.

Chapter 6

1. "Percentage of older people receiving long-term care at a residential care facility and at home," Maternal, Newborn, Child and Adolescent Health and Ageing Data Portal, World Health Organization, accessed September 27, 2023, https://www.who.int/data/maternal-newborn-child-adolescent-ageing/indicator-explorer-new/mca/percentage-of-older-people-receiving-long-term-care-at-a-residential-care-facility-and-at-home.

"Access to long-term care," Health at a Glance 2021, OECD iLibrary, accessed September 27, 2023, https://www.oecd-ilibrary.org/social-issues-migration-health/health-at-a-glance-2021_4c4694a2-en.

Institute of Medicine (US) Food Forum, *Providing Healthy and Safe Foods As We Age: Workshop Summary* (Washington, DC: National Academies Press, 2010), https://www.ncbi.nlm.nih.gov/books/nbk51841.

"A portrait of Canada's growing population aged 85 and older from the 2021 Census," 2021 Census of Population, Statistics Canada, last modified April 27, 2022, https://www12.statcan.gc.ca/census-recensement/2021/as-sa/98-200-x/2021004/98-200-x2021004-eng.cfm.

Chapter 8

1. Kathleen C. Insel and Terry A. Badger, "Deciphering the 4 D's: cognitive decline, delirium, depression and dementia—a review," *Journal of Advanced Nursing* 38, no. 4 (May 2002): 360–8, https://doi.org/10.1046/j.1365-2648.2002.02196.x.

2. Alzheimer's Association, *2023 Alzheimer's Disease Facts and Figures* (Chicago: Alzheimer's Association, March 2023), https://doi.org/10.1002/alz.13016.

"Dementia in Canada: Summary," Canadian Institute for Health Information, accessed September 27, 2023, https://www.cihi.ca/en/dementia-in-canada/dementia-in-canada-summary.

3. "Dementia," World Health Organization, last modified March 15, 2023, https://www.who.int/news-room/fact-sheets/detail/dementia.

4. For a great overview of causes of dementia, including the role of genetics, see:

"Genes and Dementia," Alzheimer's Research UK, last modified November 2022, https://www.alzheimersresearchuk.org/dementia-information/genes-and-dementia.

5. "Dementia," World Health Organization, last modified March 15, 2023, https://www.who.int/news-room/fact-sheets/detail/dementia.

6. Alzheimer's Association, *2023 Alzheimer's Disease Facts and Figures* (Chicago: Alzheimer's Association, March 2023), https://doi.org/10.1002/alz.13016.

7. Ibid.

8. "Dementia," World Health Organization, last modified March 15, 2023, https://www.who.int/news-room/fact-sheets/detail/dementia.

9. Chandrani Dutta et al., "Urinary Tract Infection Induced Delirium in Elderly Patients: A Systematic Review," *Cureus* 14, no. 12, (December 2022): e32321, https://doi.org/10.7759/cureus.32321.

"Urinary tract infections and dementia," Alzheimer's Society, accessed September 28, 2023, https://www.alzheimers.org.uk/get-support/daily-living/urinary-tract-infections-utis-dementia.

10. Malinee Neelamegam et al., "The effect of opioids on the cognitive function of older adults: results from the Personality and Total Health through life study," *Age and Ageing* 50, no. 5, (September 2021): 1699–1708, https://doi.org/10.1093/ageing/afab048.

"Prescription Opioids DrugFacts," National Institute on Drug Abuse, accessed July 19, 2023, https://nida.nih.gov/publications/drugfacts/prescription-opioids.

For a broader, easier-to-read overview of medications that can affect cognition, see: "Caution! These Drugs Can Cause Memory Loss," AARP, last modified April 14, 2023, https://www.aarp.org/health/drugs-supplements/info-2017/caution-these-10-drugs-can-cause-memory-loss.html.

11. Michelle Crouch, "6 Medical Problems That Can Mimic Dementia—but Aren't," AARP, last modified April 25, 2023, https://www.aarp.org/health/conditions-treatments/info-2022/medical-problems-mimic-dementia.html.

12. Elizabeth K. Rhodus et al., "Behaviors Characteristic of Autism Spectrum Disorder in a Geriatric Cohort With Mild Cognitive Impairment or Early Dementia," *Alzheimer Disease & Associated Disorders* 34, no. 1, (January–March 2020): 66–71, https://doi.org/10.1097/WAD.0000000000000345.

13. Renee P. Meyer and Dean Schuyler, "Posttraumatic Stress Disorder and Dementia," *The Primary Care Companion for CNS Disorders* 16, no. 5, (October 2014) https://doi.org/10.4088/PCC.14f01701.

14. S. Hoops et al., "Validity of the MoCA and MMSE in the detection of MCI and dementia in Parkinson disease," *Neurology* 73, no. 21, (November 2009): 1738–1745, https://doi.org/10.1212/WNL.0b013e3181c34b47.

Chapter 9

1. Alzheimer's Disease International and Karolinska Institutet, *Global Estimates of Informal Care* (London: Alzheimer's Disease International, July 2018), https://www.alzint.org/u/global-estimates-of-informal-care.pdf.

"Dementia in home and community care," Canadian Institute for Health Information, accessed July 19, 2023, https://www.cihi.ca/en/dementia-in-canada/dementia-care-across-the-health-system/dementia-in-home-and-community-care.

2. "Music-Memory Connection Found in Brain," Jeremy Hsu, Live Science, last modified February 24, 2009, https://www.livescience.com/5327-music-memory-connection-brain.html.

Music can be used as a form of therapy, and playing a person with dementia's favorite songs can decrease agitation: Huei-Chuan Sung and Anne M. Chang, "Use of preferred music to decrease agitated behaviours in older people with dementia: a review of the literature," *Journal of Clinical Nursing* 14, no. 9, (October 2005): 1133–40, https://doi.org/10.1111/j.1365-2702.2005.01218.x.

Chapter 10

1. Karen M. Detering et al., "The impact of advance care planning on end of life care in elderly patients: randomised controlled trial," *BMJ* (March 2010): 340, https://doi.org/10.1136/bmj.c1345.

I think the Canadian data is quite overestimated at 30 to 40 percent: "Canadians and their Money: Key Findings from the 2019 Canadian Financial Capability Survey," Financial Consumer Agency of Canada, last modified January 31, 2023, https://www.canada.ca/en/financial-consumer-agency/programs/research/canadian-financial-capability-survey-2019.html.

In Australia, it's a dismal 11 percent for many types of POA: "The NHMRC Partnership Centre on Dealing with Cognitive and Related Functional Decline in Older People," *The Policies and Practices of Financial Institutions Around Substitute Decision Making* (Sydney: Cognitive Decline Partnership Centre, June 2019), https://cdpc.sydney.edu.au/wp-content/uploads/2019/06/final-report-policies-practices-of-financial-institutions.pdf.

Chapter 13

1. "New FTC Data Show Consumers Reported Losing Nearly $8.8 Billion to Scams in 2022," Federal Trade Commission, February 23, 2023, ftc.gov/news-events/news/press-releases/2023/02/new-ftc-data-show-consumers-reported-losing-nearly-88-billion-scams-2022.
2. This section draws heavily from work we have done at CanAge on "Senior Smart" training materials. My thanks to the CanAge team and to Karen Rosen and Meg Lauber for their contributions.

Chapter 14

1. Carolyn Zahn-Waxler and Grazyna Kochanska, "The origins of guilt," in *Nebraska Symposium on Motivation, 1988*, ed. Ross A. Thompson (Lincoln: University of Nebraska Press, 1990), 183–258.
2. Libing Shen, "The evolution of shame and guilt," *PLOS One* 13, no. 7, (July 2018): e0199448, http://doi.org/10.1371/journal.pone.0199448.
3. "How to Deal with Guilt So It Doesn't Drag You Down," Kimberly Drake, PsychCentral, last modified March 25, 2022, https://psychcentral.com/health/tips-for-dealing-with-guilt.

Chapter 15

1. There are numerous studies that show these astonishing results. For an elegant overview of these positive intergenerational health impacts, see: Stanford Center on Longevity, *Hidden in Plain Sight: How Intergenerational Relationships Can Transform Our Future*, June 2016, https://longevity.stanford.edu/hidden-in-plain-sight-how-intergenerational-relationships-can-transform-our-future.
2. Sara M. Moorman and Jeffrey E. Stokes, "Solidarity in the Grandparent–Adult Grandchild Relationship and Trajectories of Depressive Symptoms," *Gerontologist* 56, no. 3 (June 2016): 408–20, https://doi.org/10.1093/geront/gnu056.

"Family Matters: Grandparents in Canada," Statistics Canada, last modified February 7, 2019, https://www150.statcan.gc.ca/n1/pub/11-627-m/11-627-m2019001-eng.htm.

Mathilde Duflos, Caroline Giraudeau, and Claude Ferrand, "What is emotional closeness between grandparents and their adolescent and emerging adult grandchildren? A systematic review," *Journal of Family Studies* 28, no. 2 (April 2020): 762–84, https://doi.org/10.1080/13229400.2020.1752771.

Chapter 16

1. Susan L. Brown and I-Fen Lin, "The Graying of Divorce: A Half Century of Change," *The Journals of Gerontology, Series B: Psychological Sciences and Social Sciences* 77, no. 9, (September 2022): 1710–20, https://doi.org/10.1093/geronb/gbac057.

"Gray Divorce: A Growing Risk Regardless of Class or Education," Susan L. Brown and I-Fen Lin, Council on Contemporary Families, accessed September 28, 2023, https://sites.utexas.edu/contemporaryfamilies/2014/10/08/growing-risk-brief-report.

Chapter 17

1. Erica Solway et al., *Let's Talk About Sex* (Ann Arbor: University of Michigan National Poll on Healthy Aging, May 2018), https://www.healthyagingpoll.org/reports-more/report/lets-talk-about-sex.

2. Amelia Portellos, Claire Lynch, and Annette Joosten, "Sexuality and ageing: A mixed methods explorative study of older adult's experiences, attitudes, and support needs," *British Journal of Occupational Therapy* 86, no. 7 (April 2023), https://doi.org/10.1177/03080226231164277.

Lee Smith et al., "Sexual Activity is Associated with Greater Enjoyment of Life in Older Adults," *Sexual Medicine* 7, no. 1 (December 2018): 11–8, https://doi.org/10.1016/j.esxm.2018.11.001.

3. Katarzyna Skałacka and Rafał Gerymski, "Sexual activity and life satisfaction in older adults," *Psychogeriatrics* 19, no. 3 (May 2019): 195–201, https://doi.org/10.1111/psyg.12381.

4. Centers for Disease Control and Prevention, *Sexually Transmitted Disease Surveillance 2019* (Atlanta: U.S. Department of Health and Human Services, April 2021), https://www.cdc.gov/std/statistics/2019/std-surveillance-2019.pdf.

5. Vanessa Schick et al., "Sexual behaviors, condom use, and sexual health of Americans over 50: implications for sexual health promotion for older adults," *Journal of Sexual Medicine* 7, no. 5 (October 2010): 315–29, https://doi.org/10.1111/j.1743-6109.2010.02013.x.

Chapter 19

1. Audrey Nelson, "Why You Stand Side-by-Side or Face-to-Face," *Psychology Today*, last modified April 27, 2014, https://www.psychologytoday.com/intl/blog/he-speaks-she-speaks/201404/why-you-stand-side-by-side-or-face-to-face.

Chapter 21

1. National Center for Health Statistics, *Mortality in the United States, 2018* (Washington, DC: U.S. Department of Health and Human Services, January 2020), https://www.cdc.gov/nchs/data/databriefs/db355-h.pdf.

2. "Coronary Artery Disease (CAD)," Centers for Disease Control and Prevention, last modified July 19, 2021, https://www.cdc.gov/heartdisease/coronary_ad.htm.

3. "Coronary Heart Disease," National Heart, Lung, and Blood Institute, last modified March 24, 2022, https://www.nhlbi.nih.gov/health/coronary-heart-disease/symptoms.

4. "Stroke: Signs, Causes, and Treatment," National Institute on Aging, last modified February 9, 2023, https://www.nia.nih.gov/health/stroke.

5. "Spot a Stroke Fast Road Sign," American Stroke Association, last modified 2019, https://www.stroke.org/en/help-and-support/resource-library/fast-materials/fast-roadsign-poster.

6. American Stroke Association, *Life After Stroke* (New York: American Heart Association, 2019), https://www.stroke.org/-/media/stroke-files/life-after-stroke/life-after-stroke-guide_7819.pdf.

7. "Which diseases cause the most death in the US?," Medical News Today, last modified June 26, 2020, https://www.medicalnewstoday.com/articles/deadliest-diseases.

Chapter 22

1. "Deafness and hearing loss," World Health Organization, last modified February 27, 2023, https://www.who.int/news-room/fact-sheets/detail/deafness-and-hearing-loss.

2. "Quick Statistics About Hearing," National Institute on Deafness and Other Communication Disorders, last modified March 25, 2021, https://www.nidcd.nih.gov/health/statistics/quick-statistics-hearing.

3. Pamela L. Ramage-Morin et al., "Unperceived hearing loss among Canadians aged 40 to 79," *Health Reports Statistics Canada* 30, no. 8, (August 2019): 11–20, https://doi.org/10.25318/82-003-x201900800002-eng.

4. Amber Willink, Nicholas S. Reed, and Frank R. Lin, "Access to Hearing Care Services Among Older Medicare Beneficiaries Using Hearing Aids," *Health Affairs* 38, no. 1 (January 2019): 124–31, https://doi.org/10.1377/hlthaff.2018.05217.

President's Council of Advisors on Science and Technology, *Aging America & Hearing Loss: Imperative of Improved Hearing Technologies*, October 2015, https://obamawhitehouse.archives.gov/sites/default/files/microsites/ostp/pcast/pcast%20hearing%20letter%20report.pdf.

5. "Hearing aids: How to choose the right one," Mayo Clinic, last modified September 20, 2022, https://www.mayoclinic.org/diseases-conditions/hearing-loss/in-depth/hearing-aids/art-20044116.

6. One good example is this guide from the National Council on Aging: https://www.ncoa.org/adviser/hearing-aids/best-hearing-aids.

7. Gill Livingston et al., "Dementia prevention, intervention, and care: 2020 report of the *Lancet* Commission," *The Lancet* 396, no. 10248 (August 2020): 413–36, https://doi.org/10.1016/S0140-6736(20)30367-6.

8. Harrison W. Lin, Hossein Mahboubi, and Neil Bhattacharyya, "Self-reported Hearing Difficulty and Risk of Accidental Injury in US Adults, 2007 to 2015," *JAMA Otolaryngology–Head & Neck Surgery*, 144, no. 5 (May 2018): 413–7, https://doi.org/10.1001/jamaoto.2018.0039.

Chapter 23

1. "Nearsightedness," Mayo Clinic, last modified September 16, 2022, https://www.mayoclinic.org/diseases-conditions/nearsightedness/symptoms-causes/syc-20375556.

2. "Glaucoma," Canadian Association of Optometrists, last modified March 28, 2023, https://opto.ca/eye-health-library/glaucoma.

3. Remo Susanna Jr. et al., "Why Do People (Still) Go Blind from Glaucoma?" *Translational Vision Science and Technology* 4, no. 2 (March 2015): 1, https://doi.org/10.1167/tvst.4.2.1.

4. "What Is a Glaucoma Drainage Implant?," American Academy of Ophthalmology, last modified May 10, 2023, https://www.aao.org/eye-health/diseases/glaucoma-drainage-implants.

5. "What Is Macular Degeneration?," American Academy of Ophthalmology, last modified April 6, 2023, https://www.aao.org/eye-health/diseases/amd-macular-degeneration.

6. "Seniors and Aging—Vision Care," Government of Canada, last modified April 4, 2017, https://www.canada.ca/en/health-canada/services/healthy-living/your-health/lifestyles/seniors-aging-vision-care.html.

7. "Cataracts," Mayo Clinic, last modified September 28, 2023, https://www.mayoclinic.org/diseases-conditions/cataracts/symptoms-causes-syc-20353790.

8. "Diabetic retinopathy," Mayo Clinic, last modified February 21, 2023, https://www.mayoclinic.org/diseases-conditions/diabetic-retinopathy/symptoms-causes/syc-20371611.

Chapter 24

1. This section draws from a great paper produced by CanAge. I wish to gratefully acknowledge the work of Diana Cable, Sarah Pillersdorf, Vanessa Sparks, and some of the other members of the Policy and Advocacy Team, whom I'm essentially ripping off here: CanAge, *Urinary Incontinence: The Impact on the Well-being of Older Adults* (Toronto: CanAge, September 2021), https://www.canage.ca/wp-content/uploads/2021/10/UTI-Paper-4-Incontinence_FINAL.pdf.

2. Sedighe Batmani et al., "Prevalence and factors related to urinary incontinence in older adult women worldwide: a comprehensive systematic review and meta-analysis of observational studies," *BMC Geriatrics* 21, no. 1 (March 2021): 212, https://doi.org/10.1186/s12877-021-02135-8.

Tatyana A. Shamliyan et al., "Male urinary incontinence: prevalence, risk factors, and preventive interventions," *Reviews in Urology* 11, no. 3 (Summer 2009): 145–65, https://pubmed.ncbi.nlm.nih.gov/19918340.

William Gibson et al., "Incontinence in frail elderly persons: Report of the 6th International Consultation on Incontinence," *Neurourology and Urodynamics* 40, no. 1 (January 2021): 38–54, https://doi.org/10.1002/nau.24549.

3. Carolyn Swenson et al., *Urinary Incontinence: An Inevitable Part of Aging?* (Ann Arbor: University of Michigan National Poll on Healthy Aging, November 2018), https://www.healthyagingpoll.org/reports-more/report/urinary-incontinence-inevitable-part-aging.

4. "Fecal incontinence," Mayo Clinic, last modified November 3, 2022, https://www.mayoclinic.org/diseases-conditions/fecal-incontinence/symptoms-causes/syc-20351397.

5. "Diarrhea," WebMD, last modified January 4, 2023, https://www.webmd.com/digestive-disorders/digestive-diseases-diarrhea.

6. "10 ways to stop leaks," National Health Service, last modified June 15, 2023, https://www.nhs.uk/conditions/urinary-incontinence/10-ways-to-stop-leaks.

"Incontinence Patient Guide," Urology Care Foundation, October 2020, https://www.urologyhealth.org/educational-resources/incontinence-x3022.

"Bladder Control: Incontinence Patient Guide," Urology Care Foundation, 2020, https://www.urologyhealth.org/educational-resources/incontinence-x3022.

7. "Diarrhea," WebMD, last modified January 4, 2023, https://www.webmd.com/digestive-disorders/digestive-diseases-diarrhea.

Chapter 25

1. "Facts About Aging and Alcohol," National Institute on Aging, last modified July 19, 2022, https://www.nia.nih.gov/health/facts-about-aging-and-alcohol.

2. Alexis Kuerbis et al., "Substance Abuse Among Older Adults," *Clinics in Geriatric Medicine* 30, no. 3 (August 2014): 629–54, https://doi.org/10.1016/j.cger.2014.04.008.

3. "Alcohol Use in Older Adults," Centre for Addiction and Mental Health, accessed September 28, 2023, https://www.camh.ca/en/health-info/guides-and-publications/alcohol-use-in-older-adults.

4. Luc Letenneur, "Risk of dementia and alcohol and wine consumption: a review of recent results," *Biological Research* 37, no. 2 (2004): 189–93, https://doi.org/10.4067/s0716-97602004000200003.

5 George F. Koob, "Age, Alcohol Use, and Brain Function: Yoda Says, 'With Age and Alcohol, Confused Is the Force,'" *JAMA Psychiatry* 75, no. 5 (May 2018): 422, https://doi.org/10.1001/jamapsychiatry.2018.0009.

6. "Alcohol and the Aging Brain," National Institute on Alcohol Abuse and Alcoholism, last modified September 13, 2018, https://niaaa.scienceblog.com/103/alcohol-and-the-aging-brain.

7. Ibid.

Chapter 26

1. Craig M. Hales et al., "Prescription Drug Use Among Adults Aged 40-79 in the United States and Canada," National Center for Health Statistics Data Brief, no. 347 (Hyattsville, MD: National Center for Health Statistics August 2019), https://www.cdc.gov/nchs/products/databriefs/db347.htm.

2. "Drug use among seniors in Canada," Canadian Institute for Health Information, accessed May 9, 2023, https://www.cihi.ca/en/drug-use-among-seniors-in-canada.

3. "Grapefruit Juice and Some Drugs Don't Mix," U.S. Food and Drug Administration, last modified July 1, 2021, https://www.fda.gov/consumers/consumer-updates/grapefruit-juice-and-some-drugs-dont-mix.

Chapter 27

1. "Older drivers," Insurance Institute for Highway Safety, last modified June 2023, https://www.iihs.org/topics/older-drivers.

Acknowledgments

To my kids, Alex Watts, Maddie Watts, and Isaac Tamblyn. Also, hey kids—I've written you a guidebook for how to handle me when you are older. Good luck, you're going to need it. I plan on being deeply difficult as I age, so buckle up.

To Jana Ray, Diana Cable, Huma Khan, Michelle Saunders, and the CanAge team. You are the backbone of it all. It's impossible to express the depth of my gratitude for everything you have done and everything you do.

To friends and colleagues who pushed me to write this book and never let me put down the proverbial pen, including but absolutely in no way limited to Dr. Raza Mirza, Krista James, Dr. Amanda Grenier, Jennifer Jones, Amy Coupal, Emma Lundgren, Jane Meadus, Moira Welsh, Andre Picard, Marta Hajek, Raeann Rideout, Heather Kiemele, Kahir Lalji, James Janiero, Dr. Esme Fuller-Thomson, Kim Whaley, Leanne Kaufman, M.T. Connolly, Dr. Deb Whitman, Dr. Jane Barratt, Dr. Alex Mihailidis, Dr. Stephen Katz, the OSCAR Roundtable members, Sarah MacLachlan, Noah Richler, Virginia Puddicombe, Suzanne Smith, Sandra Cunningham, and the incredible village community of Sandy Cove, NS. Special love and gratitude are sent to Dr. Karen Kobayashi, who passed away during the writing of this book.

To my agents Sam Haywood and Rob Firing. Thank you for never giving up on this book even during COVID-19, when I was working flat out on the front lines and, like so many who work with seniors, was a little preoccupied with that whole pandemic thing. And to Hannah Matuszak, my brilliant and supportive editor. All errors and deeply questionable humor are entirely my own.

To those folks who gave me permission to use their stories in service of this bigger tale, thank you.

To Oprah (bet ya didn't see that one coming . . . but I absolutely don't know her any more than you do), who recently decided to take up the cause of aging, menopause, and longevity and is raising awareness of these issues for millions of people worldwide, helping them understand that we don't all age the same way with the same privileges. Leadership and giving voice to issues matter.

All resemblance to persons living or dead is purely coincidental, as I tried really hard to make sure people don't figure it out—joking! (sort of).

Index

About the Author

Laura Tamblyn Watts is the CEO of CanAge, Canada's national seniors' advocacy organization. She teaches Law and Aging at the University of Toronto and has worked as a lawyer defending the rights of older people. Tamblyn Watts is also a regular media guest and keynote speaker on aging issues. She lives in Toronto, Canada.

canage.ca | @ltamblynwatts